SOYA FOODS COOKERY

The Author

Born in the USA, Leah Leneman has lived in Britain for more than twenty years. She spent several years working for British Airways, and travelled extensively. At one time Assistant Editor of *The Vegetarian*, she now writes vegetarian cookery books and articles on a freelance basis. Her previous books include *Slimming the Vegetarian Way* (1980), *Vegan Cooking* (1982), *The Amazing Avocado* (1984), *The International Tofu Cookery Book* (1986) and *Vegetarian Pitta Bread Recipes* (1987).

SOYA FOODS COOKERY

Leah Leneman

ROUTLEDGE & KEGAN PAUL
London and New York

First published in 1988 by
Routledge & Kegan Paul Ltd
11 New Fetter Lane, London EC4P 4EE

Published in the USA by
Routledge & Kegan Paul Inc.
in association with Methuen Inc.
29 West 35th Street, New York, NY 10001

Set in Garamond 12/13pt
by Columns of Reading
and printed in the British Isles
by The Guernsey Press Co Ltd
Guernsey, Channel Islands

© *Leah Leneman 1988*

No part of this book may be reproduced in
any form without permission from the publisher
except for the quotation of brief passages
in criticism

Library of Congress Cataloging in Publication Data
Leneman, Leah.
Soya foods cookery.
Includes index.
1. Cookery (Soybeans)   2. Cookery (Tofu)   I. Title.
TX803.S6L46   1988   641.6'5655   87-13982
ISBN 0-7102-1028-0

British Library CIP Data also available

ISBN 0-7102-1028-0

Text design and illustrations
by Lucy Allen

CONTENTS

Introduction vii

I SOYA MILK 1
1 Soya milk 3
2 Soya yogurt, soft cheese and mayonnaise 5
3 Soya milk skin 9

II TOFU 19
1 Tofu 21
2 Frozen and dried-frozen tofu 52
3 Smoked tofu 68

III TEMPEH 83

IV MISO 103

V COMBI-DISHES 121
1 Tofu and miso 123
2 Tempeh and tofu 132

Index 142

INTRODUCTION

Everyone knows that soya beans are packed with protein, and here are some facts and figures: soya beans contain all eight essential amino acids and about 35 percent high-quality protein – more than any other plant or vegetable food, and they are free of saturated fats and cholesterol. Not everyone realizes that only a small percentage of the world's soya bean crop is eaten directly by human beings, the bulk of it being used as animal feed – the most horrifying waste of global resources imaginable.

Soya oil, soya flour, and some other soya products such as lecithin (used as an emulsifier in chocolate and other foods) find their way into a large number of processed foods, but one could hardly claim that this is making real use of the nutritive potential of soya beans. One way in which soya beans are consumed is as textured vegetable protein, a high-technology product made to simulate the taste and texture of meat, and found in many health food stores.

The main problem which many people find when, full of enthusiasm, they first cook soya beans (and, unfortunately, this can go for soya flour and TVP as well) is how difficult they are to digest. Quite frankly, anyone prone to flatulence would be well advised not to try eating the bean in its 'natural' state. Fortunately, once the bean has been made into a milk, curdled into tofu, or fermented into miso or tempeh, this ceases to be a problem; indeed, they are wonderfully easy to digest.

Most people are familiar with soya sauce, a readily available flavouring which also falls into the category of fermented soya foods. It is worth pointing out here that many commercial brands found on supermarket shelves contain undesirable additives, so when buying from such a source the label should be carefully perused. Health food and wholefood shops sell natural soya sauce, usually labelled 'Tamari' or 'Shoyu' (the difference between the two is of no real concern). Soya sauce is easy to accept because everyone has encountered it in Chinese food. Other soya foods may appeal to you, but you may not know how to use them. They certainly are incredibly versatile foods, and a cookery book like this can only begin to suggest some of the myriad delicious ways of making them a regular part of your diet.

Quantities

The recipes are all meant to serve four people.

American measurements

The quantities in brackets are American 8-ounce cups (not British cups, which are 10 fluid ounces). American cooks should note that British spoon measurements are about one-quarter larger than American, and adjust quantities accordingly.

Table of metric equivalents

One ounce is equivalent to 28 grams, which can add up to very awkward amounts if used literally. Below is a simplified table of equivalents for those who prefer to weigh things metrically.

1 oz = 25 gm	11 oz = 300 gm
2 oz = 50 gm	12 oz = 350 gm
3 oz = 75 gm	13 oz = 375 gm
4 oz = 100 gm	14 oz = 400 gm
5 oz = 150 gm	15 oz = 425 gm
6 oz = 175 gm	1 lb = 450 gm
7 oz = 200 gm	
8 oz = 225 gm	
9 oz = 250 gm	½ pint = 275 ml
10 oz = 275 gm	1 pint = 575 ml

Part One

SOYA MILK

· 1 ·
Soya milk

Many years ago, when I worked at Cranks Restaurant, I remember an American looking very puzzled as he read, amongst the list of beverages, 'cows' milk'. Finally light dawned – 'Oh, *milk*', he said; it had obviously never occurred to him that milk actually came from a cow. One thing is certain: animals, other than domestic pets, do not normally drink the milk of another species, or any milk at all after they pass a certain age. Cows' milk is very different in composition from human milk, containing a higher fat and protein content, and modern Western men and women have suffered in health because of their dependence on the milk of the cow.

In the Far East lactose-intolerance is very prevalent, and the traditional diet there does not include dairy produce. Milk is certainly not necessary in the diet, and I once heard a very smug vegan speaker reply, when asked about alternatives to cows' milk, that *he'd* been weaned. The fact remains, however, that in the West we are accustomed to milk, used to having it over our breakfast cereal, in our custard, in cakes, in oh-so-many of our dishes. Soya milk can be used in exactly the same way as dairy milk and is much healthier and its production does not cause distress to animals. It is easy to digest because the fibrous part of the bean has been removed; it is high in protein, low in fat and calories and free of cholesterol.

Soya milk

In recent years there has been a boom in soya milks, and there is now a good choice of brands. These include some which are completely unsweetened, and others which are sweetened with raw sugar, honey, or barley malt. There are also flavoured milks. If, therefore, the first time you try soya milk you are not keen on it, it is well worth sampling different kinds until you find the one best suited to your taste buds. Most soya milks these days come ready to drink in cartons, but there are also some concentrated varieties, and some powdered milks, which are particularly useful for anyone who perhaps lives alone and does not have milk every day, because they can be made up in either large or small amounts as required.

Soya milk can be made cheaply at home, but this is one instance where the effort does not seem to me commensurate with the result, so I do not propose to provide instructions here. Nor does there seem much point in providing specific recipes, when there are already a million recipes or more calling for 'milk', where the soya variety can be used.

• 2 •
Soya yogurt, soft cheese, and mayonnaise

Yogurt

It may seem surprising that the bacteria which thrive on the milk of a cow should also thrive on the milk of a bean, but so it is: soya milk makes wonderful yogurt.

Extravagant claims have been made for yogurt as a 'health' food, but it is worth noting that the 'healthy' ingredient is not the milk but the beneficial bacteria which do such wonders for the digestion. Indeed, soya yogurt is particularly valuable in a vegan diet, because it makes the high-fibre foods which are such an intrinsic part of the diet so much easier to digest.

Is yogurt vegan? The name of the commonest form of yogurt culture, *Lactobacillus bulgaricus*, may mislead some people into thinking there is a dairy derivative in it, but such is not the case; it merely indicates that the bacteria have an affinity with milk. When I first started making yogurt I feared the dried ferment which I bought at the health food store would contain some milk sugar, but I was assured by a major manufacturer that this was not so. Since then, manufacturers of yogurt ferments have started listing their ingredients, and it is clear that the majority do not contain any dairy derivatives. And if anyone is worried about bacteria being 'alive' it is worth pointing out that they are akin to the yeast used to make bread and are considered by scientists to be a lower form of life than plants.

Soya yogurt, in a variety of flavours, is becoming readily available in most British and American health food stores. It is lovely and creamy – a real winner. And the culture is guaranteed dairy-free.

Making soya yogurt at home is very easy. It is important to boil the milk first, then cool it to lukewarm. A useful guide to the temperature required is that when a finger is dipped into it, it should feel lukewarm but with a slight 'sting' of heat at about the count of ten. It is better to err on the cool than the warm side, for if the temperature is too high the bacteria will simply be killed off. From then on just follow the instructions on the packet of ferment. (NB A wide-topped vacuum flask is every bit as good as an expensive yogurt maker.) The first two or three batches tend to be rather sweet and runny, but after that they keep on getting better and better.

Yogurt can be made from any soya milk on the market. I have always used a sweetened variety, and some friends who buy only unsweetened ones add a little sugar or apple juice when making yogurt, but other friends have found they can make perfect yogurt from unsweetened soya milk.

The initial purchase of the dried ferment is rather expensive. But if one uses a spoonful of existing yogurt to make a fresh batch at least once a week (much better to make frequent small quantities than infrequent large ones), then one can keep it going for a year or more. One trick I learned when I went away on a fortnight's holiday was to freeze a couple of spoonfuls of yogurt: when defrosted the consistency was completely different, but it still worked beautifully as a ferment.

Soya yogurt can be used in the same ways as dairy yogurt. So many Indian and Middle-Eastern vegetarian cookery books provide recipes incorporating yogurt and requiring no other adaptation that it seems pointless to add specific recipes here.

Soft cheese

I have been told that kits sold for making soft cheese work very well with soya milk. I have not bought one, for the simple reason that soft cheese is much more limited in its uses than yogurt, so that I could not keep it going constantly, and buying new ferment each time would be expensive. A kit could certainly prove a useful investment for a catering business or restaurant, though.

If I want a soft cheese I simply pour yogurt into a large square of muslin and tie it up to drip for several hours or overnight. Quite a large quantity of yogurt is needed to make rather a small quantity of cheese, but it really is lovely and can be flavoured in a number of different ways (e.g. with chives for a savoury spread or pineapple for a sweet spread).

Mayonnaise

Recipes are available for making a mayonnaise-type dressing from soya flour and from dried soya milk, but I have never found the results particularly satisfactory, so such recipes do not appear in this book. The simplest way to make a mayonnaise-type dressing at home is to put some tofu (either Morinaga Silken Tofu or firm tofu, though if using the latter a little soya milk may also be required) into a liquidizer with a little oil and lemon juice and blend thoroughly, adding any additional flavourings desired. The proportions are not important: it's best to add the other ingredients to the tofu a little at a time until the right taste and consistency are reached.

At time of writing, there are two soya-based dressings available at health food stores and speciality shops in the UK, both made by St Giles Foods Ltd, Sandhurst Road, Sidcup, Kent: 'Duchesse' Tofu Dressing and Dip and 'Life' Mayonnaise Style Dressing, which is free of salt and sugar. Similar soya-based dressings are available widely in the USA.

· 3 ·
Soya milk skin

When soya milk boils it forms a skin on top in the same way as dairy milk, the difference being that soya milk skin is substantial enough to be skimmed off as a food in its own right. In Japan fresh *yuba*, as it is called there, is very popular, and it is certainly a very valuable food, containing all the goodness of soya milk.

To the best of my knowledge, one cannot buy this product fresh in the UK, but Chinese shops sell a dried version, both in 'sticks' and in 'sheets'. To confuse the uninitiated, these products are usually labelled 'dried bean curd', so that anyone looking for dried tofu (see Part 2, Section 2) may be misled into thinking that is what they are buying. Soya milk in China is generally made to be curdled into tofu, and therefore soya milk skin is associated in people's minds with bean curd, though it is in fact skimmed off before the milk is curdled.

This dried skin, when rehydrated, has a pleasantly chewy texture, and I have provided two traditional Chinese recipes using the sticks in their natural form. However, the main use for it in China is in vegetarian Buddhist temple cookery, where it is used to simulate various meat dishes. I am not qualified to judge how much resemblance they bear to the 'originals'; all I know is that the recipes of this kind which I have included are very tasty in their own right.

Soya milk

The only reason I have not provided more recipes using this food – which I think has terrific potential in Western vegetarian cuisine (it is much easier to digest than TVP and has no beany aftertaste) – is because they tend on the whole to be rather fiddly and time-consuming. On the one occasion when I tried to simplify a traditional recipe by using shortcuts the result was a culinary disaster, at which point it seemed best to quit while I was ahead.

Stir-fried bean milk sticks Shanghai-style

2 oz dried mushrooms
8 oz dried bean milk sticks
4 oz bamboo shoots
3 tablespoons vegetable oil
8 oz cooked asparagus
2 teaspoons sea salt
3 tablespoons cider vinegar
4 tablespoons soya sauce
2 tablespoons brown sugar
Pinch of five-spice powder
2 teaspoons cornflour dissolved in 2 tablespoons water
Brown rice as required

Cover the mushrooms with warm water and leave to soak for about half an hour.

Break the bean milk sticks into 2-inch pieces and soak them in warm water for about half an hour. (NB There will almost invariably be some pieces that will remain hard; it is best to discard those.)

Drain and chop the mushrooms, discarding the stem. If the bamboo shoots are not already sliced then slice them thinly.

Heat the oil in a wok or frying pan, and stir-fry the drained bean milk pieces, bamboo shoots and mushrooms for 2-3 minutes. Stir in the asparagus and seasonings and cook for a minute or two longer (being careful not to break the asparagus). Finally, stir in the cornflour and water and stir until thickened.

Serve immediately over brown rice.

Pancakes stuffed with bean milk sticks

8 oz dried bean milk sticks
8 oz mushrooms
3 tablespoons vegetable oil + extra as rqrd
1 small tin bamboo shoots
6 tablespoons soya sauce
3 teaspoons brown sugar
4 tablespoons sesame oil
8 oz (2 cups) wholemeal flour
Pinch sea salt

Cover the bean milk sticks with lots of warm water, and soak for half an hour or more until the sticks have softened. Drain well and chop coarsely.

Chop the mushrooms.

Heat the 3 tablespoons vegetable oil in a wok or frying pan and add the chopped dried bean milk. Stir-fry for 2-3 minutes. Add the mushrooms and bamboo shoots (if they are not already sliced then chop them first). Continue cooking for 2-3 minutes longer, until the mixture is fairly dry. Stir in the soya sauce and sugar and cook for another minute or two. Remove from heat and stir in 2 tablespoons sesame oil. Keep warm while making the pancakes.

To make the pancakes, mix the flour with the salt in a bowl and rub in the other 2 tablespoons sesame oil. Add enough hot water to make a soft pliable dough. Knead well and form into a long sausage. Break off small pieces and roll out as thinly as possible. Fry each pancake in a minimum of oil, turning over so that each side is browned.

Spread each pancake with some of the bean milk stick mixture and roll up. Keep warm until all are filled and ready to serve.

Mock 'ham'

8 oz dried bean milk sheets
⅓ pint (1 cup) water
4 tablespoons soya sauce
1 tablespoon cider vinegar
1 teaspoon raw sugar
1 tablespoon sesame oil

Break the sheets up into small pieces.

Combine the water, soya sauce, vinegar and sugar in a large saucepan. Add the pieces of milk skin sheets and turn them in the sauce. Bring to the boil, then lower heat and simmer for about 20 minutes until the sauce has been absorbed. Add the sesame oil.

Turn out on to a large piece of muslin and roll up the cloth into a sausage shape. Tie it up securely with lots of string. Steam it over hot water for 2 hours.

Remove from heat and leave it to cool, then chill it thoroughly in the fridge before unwrapping and slicing it. (Nice with bread and vegetable margarine, and lettuce leaves.)

• Mock 'chicken' •

3 tablespoons soya sauce
1 tablespoon raw sugar
1 tablespoon sesame oil

8 oz dried bean milk sheets
Vegetable oil for deep-frying

Heat the soya sauce, sugar and sesame oil in a small saucepan until boiling, then remove from heat and leave to cool.

Cover the bean milk sheets with hot water and leave 2-3 minutes until soft. Drain.

Lay a single sheet out on a large piece of muslin and sprinkle with a little of the sauce mixture. Cover with another sheet and more sauce until all have been used up, finishing with a layer of bean milk sheet. If the sheets are not whole but fragmented – as will very likely be the case – it doesn't matter, just make up a whole sheet of pieces without worrying at this stage about them cohering. If any pieces are tough rather than tender then discard those.

When the layers are complete roll them up in a sausage shape, inside a large piece of muslin and tie up the sausage with strong twine. Steam over hot water for 2 hours.

Remove from heat and leave it to cool. Then deep-fry it

in hot oil for 3-4 minutes (if it is not completely immersed in the oil, then it is a good idea to turn it over after 2 minutes).

Drain thoroughly, then slice and serve hot or as an ingredient in another dish. (See below.)

Mock 'chicken' cooked Indonesian style

1 onion
2 cloves garlic
1-inch piece fresh ginger
6 blanched almonds
2 tablespoons soya sauce
2 tablespoons vegetable oil
2 teaspoons ground cumin
2 teaspoons ground coriander
1 teaspoon turmeric
$\frac{1}{2}$ teaspoon (or more to taste) chilli powder
$\frac{1}{2}$ pint ($1\frac{1}{3}$ cups) water
1 oz creamed coconut
1 tablespoon cider vinegar
2 teaspoons dark brown raw sugar
Mock 'chicken' made from 8 oz soya milk skin (see recipe above)
Brown rice as required

Chop the onion, garlic and ginger. Put them into a liquidizer, food processor or mortar and pestle, along with the almonds and soya sauce, and blend into a paste. (If you are using a liquidizer some of the water will probably be necessary as well.)

Heat the oil in a saucepan and add the paste, along with the cumin, coriander, turmeric and chilli. Stir over a low to medium heat for about 2 minutes. Add the water, creamed coconut, vinegar and sugar and stir well. Bring to the boil. Slice the 'chicken' and add to the saucepan. Cover the pan and simmer over low heat for 15-20 minutes. Serve with brown rice.

• *Part Two* •

TOFU

· 1 ·
Tofu

Tofu — soya bean curd — is a nutritious and versatile food. The protein content is high; the calorie and fat content are low; the cholesterol content is nil. Because it has been curdled, it is even easier to digest than soya milk. It has very little flavour of its own but can be used in an amazing variety of ways.

Tofu can be found in Chinese shops, but the Chinese prefer a slightly 'burnt' taste to their tofu, so tofu bought in Chinese shops is much more limited in its uses. Morinaga Long-Life Silken Tofu is available at every British health food store, but though it is useful for puréed dishes, it is much less so for other things, because no matter how much one tries to firm it up, it never really holds together terribly well. The most suitable tofu for most of the recipes in this section is the firm type found in the refrigerated section of an ever-increasing number of health food and wholefood shops.

(NB Instructions for making tofu at home — as well as over a hundred additional recipes — can be found in *The International Tofu Cookery Book*, published by RKP in 1986.)

Tofu can add rich creaminess to soups, as in the recipes which follow. Either regular tofu or Silken tofu can be used.

Mushroom bisque

2 onions
2 tablespoons vegetable margarine
12 oz mushrooms
1 tablespoon paprika
$\frac{1}{4}$ teaspoon cayenne pepper
1 pint ($2\frac{1}{2}$ cups) vegetable stock or water
Sea salt and freshly ground black pepper
8 oz (1 cup) tofu
$1\frac{1}{2}$ tablespoons vegetable oil
3 teaspoons lemon juice

Chop the onions and sauté in the margarine for 4-5 minutes.

Chop the mushrooms finely and add to the saucepan with the paprika and cayenne and stir. Cover the saucepan and leave to cook for 7-10 minutes.

Stir in the stock or water and the salt and pepper, bring to the boil, and simmer for a further 3-4 minutes.

Liquidize the tofu with the oil and lemon juice. Stir the tofu mixture into the saucepan, and heat gently, without allowing it to boil. Taste and adjust seasoning if necessary. Serve immediately.

Cream of cauliflower and potato soup

1 small cauliflower
1 onion
1 lb potatoes
1½ pints (3¾ cups) water or vegetable stock
8 oz (1 cup) tofu
Sea salt and freshly ground black pepper
½ oz (⅛ cup) vegetable margarine
Minced parsley as required

Chop the cauliflower, onion, and potatoes into dice and cook in the water or stock until very soft. Cool briefly, then pour into a liquidizer along with the tofu, and blend thoroughly.

Return the mixture to the saucepan, add seasoning and the margarine, and reheat gently. Serve topped with minced parsley.

• Tomato bisque •

2 onions
2 14-oz tins tomatoes
$\frac{2}{3}$ pint (1$\frac{1}{2}$ cups) water
2 teaspoons sea salt
4 whole cloves

2 teaspoons dried dill weed (or fresh if available)
8 oz (1 cup) tofu
1 tablespoon vegetable oil

Chop the onions finely. Put into a saucepan along with the tomatoes (chopped coarsely with a spoon while adding them), the water, and the seasonings. Bring to the boil, then lower heat and simmer, uncovered, for 20-30 minutes.

Put the tofu into a liquidizer along with the oil and a few spoonfuls of liquid from the soup mixture. Blend thoroughly.

Add the contents of the liquidizer to the saucepan. Heat gently at a very low heat and serve immediately.

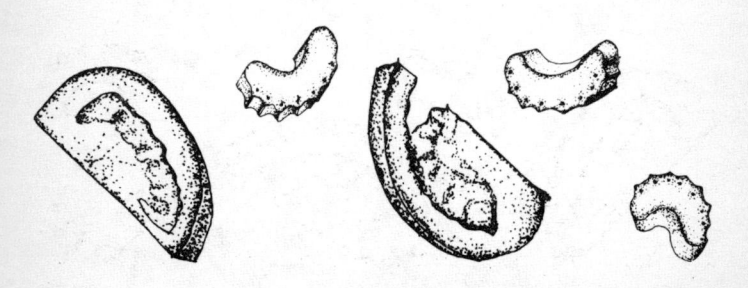

• Cream of celery soup •

1 head celery
1 onion
2 tablespoons vegetable oil
1¾ pints (4 cups) water or vegetable stock
Sea salt and freshly ground black pepper
1 teaspoon dried mixed herbs
8 oz (1 cup) tofu
2 tablespoons minced parsley

Scrub and chop the celery. Chop the onion. Sauté both in the oil for a few minutes.

Add the water or stock, seasoning and herbs. Bring to the boil, then lower heat and simmer for about 20 minutes.

Pour into the liquidizer and leave to cool slightly. Add the tofu, and blend thoroughly.

Pour back into the saucepan, and re-heat gently. Serve topped with parsley.

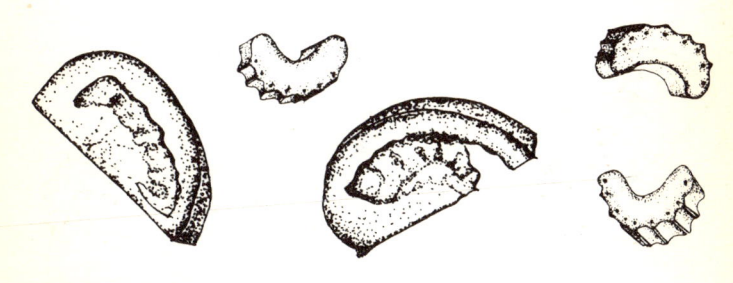

Chilled cream of cucumber soup

1 cucumber
1 onion
1 pint (2½ cups) water or vegetable stock
1 tablespoon soya sauce
8 oz (1 cup) tofu
1 tablespoon vegetable oil
Sea salt and freshly ground black pepper

Peel and dice the cucumber, keeping some back for garnish. Chop the onion.

Put the water or stock, soya sauce, cucumber and onion in a saucepan, and bring to the boil. Lower heat, cover and simmer for about 15 minutes.

Put the tofu, oil and mixture from the saucepan into a liquidizer and blend thoroughly.

Season to taste, cool, then chill. Garnish with reserved cucumber before serving.

• Vichyssoise •

4 leeks
1 onion
2 oz ($\frac{1}{4}$ cup) vegetable margarine
1 lb potatoes
1$\frac{3}{4}$ pints (4 cups) water or vegetable stock
3 tablespoons soya sauce
Freshly ground black pepper
8 oz (1 cup) tofu
Chives or spring onions (scallions) as required

Chop the leeks and onion finely. Sauté in the margarine for 5-10 minutes over low heat until nicely tender.

Peel the potatoes or leave skins on if preferred and dice them. Add them to the saucepan, along with the water or stock, the soya sauce, and the pepper. Bring to the boil, then cover and simmer for about 20 minutes, until the potatoes are soft. Cool slightly.

Put the soup mixture in the liquidizer along with the tofu, and blend thoroughly.

Chill thoroughly, and serve sprinkled with finely chopped chives or spring onions (scallions).

Deep-fried tofu makes a nice 'chewy' addition to soups.

• *Tofu gumbo soup* •

1 onion
1 small green pepper
8 oz okra
2 tablespoons vegetable oil + additional for deep-frying
8 oz (1 cup) tofu
1 14-oz tin tomatoes
1½ pints (3¾ cups) water or vegetable stock
1 bay leaf
2-3 tablespoons minced parsley
Sea salt and freshly ground black pepper

Chop the onion and green pepper. Clean the okra, top and tail them, and chop each one into 2 or 3 pieces. Sauté these ingredients in the oil for 4-5 minutes, stirring occasionally.

Chop the tofu into small dice and deep-fry until golden brown. Drain on kitchen paper.

Add the tomatoes, the water, and the bay leaf to the okra mixture, bring to the boil, then lower heat, cover and simmer for 15-20 minutes.

Add the tofu, parsley and seasoning, cook for a couple of minutes longer, and serve.

• Mulligatawny soup •

1 onion
2 sticks celery
1 carrot
1 apple
8 oz tomatoes
1 oz vegetable margarine
1-2 tablespoons curry powder
2 cloves
1 tablespoon chopped parsley
1½ pints (3¾ cups) water
1 teaspoon yeast extract
4 oz (½ cup) tofu
Vegetable oil for deep-frying
¼ pint (⅔ cup) soya milk
3 tablespoons wholemeal flour
Sea salt and freshly ground black pepper

Chop the onion, celery and carrot finely. Peel and chop the apple; skin the tomatoes and chop them. Fry all these ingredients in the margarine for about 5 minutes.

Stir in the curry powder and cook for a further minute or two. Add the cloves, parsley, water and yeast extract. Bring to the boil, then lower heat and simmer for about half an hour.

Meanwhile, chop the tofu into small dice and deep-fry until golden. Drain well.

Mix the soya milk and flour together.

Pour half the contents of the saucepan into the liquidizer and blend thoroughly. Return to the saucepan. Add the milk and flour mixture and stir well. Add the tofu cubes, season, heat thoroughly and serve.

Tofu can be used to make a variety of spreads and dips, as shown by the two examples below.

• *Devilled tofu and celery spread* •

1 lb (2 cups) tofu
4 sticks celery
4 tablespoons 'Duchesse' Sandwich Spread*
½ teaspoon paprika
1 teaspoon garlic salt
3 teaspoons soya sauce

1 teaspoon ground coriander
1 teaspoon ground cumin
1 teaspoon curry powder
3 teaspoons made mustard

Mash the tofu. Chop the celery finely.

Combine all ingredients in a mixing bowl, and serve chilled on hot toast or in sandwiches.

---

* Available in some health food shops & delicatessens. Made by St Giles Foods Ltd, Sandhurst Road, Sidcup, Kent.

• Creamy bean dip •

2 15-oz tins red kidney beans
Juice of 1 small or ½ large lemon
2 teaspoons ground cumin
1 teaspoon chilli powder
3-4 spring onions (scallions)
8 oz (2 cups) tofu
2 tablespoons olive oil
2 teaspoons oregano
½ teaspoon garlic salt

Drain the beans, reserving some of the liquid.

Put all the ingredients into a liquidizer and blend, adding enough bean liquid to get the desired consistency. (The mixture can either be blended very thoroughly to make a smooth dip, or less thoroughly to make a rougher-textured dip.)

Tofu

Tofu can be used in a wide range of savoury dishes.

• *Spicy tofu with coconut sauce* •

$1\frac{1}{4}$-$1\frac{1}{2}$ lb ($2\frac{1}{2}$-3 cups) firm tofu
2 tablespoons whole coriander seeds
$\frac{1}{4}$ teaspoon whole fenugreek seeds
1 teaspoon whole black peppercorns
10 dried curry leaves
1 onion
3 cloves garlic
2 tablespoons vegetable oil
1 teaspoon whole black mustard seeds
1 teaspoon finely grated fresh ginger
2 tablespoons paprika
$\frac{3}{4}$ teaspoon chilli powder
$\frac{1}{2}$ teaspoon turmeric
Sea salt to taste
2 teaspoons lemon juice
2 whole fresh green chillies
$\frac{3}{4}$ pint (2 cups) water
6 oz ($\frac{3}{4}$ cup) creamed coconut
Brown rice as required

Drain the tofu well. Cube and set aside.

Heat a small cast-iron frying pan over a medium flame, then put in the coriander and fenugreek seeds and the peppercorns. Stir them for about a minute or so until they are lightly roasted. Remove from the heat. Put them in a liquidizer and grind along with the curry leaves as finely as possible.

Slice the onion thinly and chop the garlic. Heat the oil in a pan and put in the mustard seeds. As soon as they begin to pop add the onion and garlic. Cook them over a medium flame until lightly browned. Stir in the ginger, then add the paprika, chilli powder, turmeric, salt, lemon juice, whole chillies and the ground spice mixture. Add the water, bring to the boil, then lower heat and simmer for 5 minutes.

Turn up the heat and add the tofu cubes. Stir them for 2-3 minutes or until they are well heated. Grate the creamed coconut and add it to the pan. Stir it in until well dissolved.

Remove the chillies and serve over brown rice.

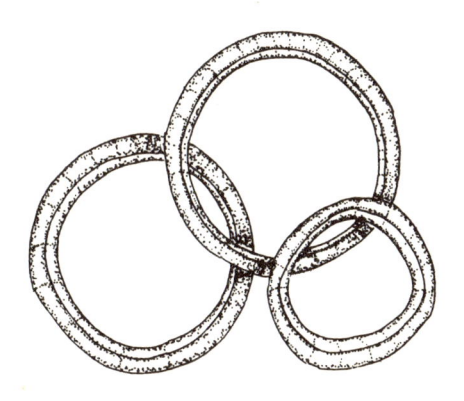

• Baked tofu slices •

1½ lb (3 cups) tofu
3 oz (¾ cup) maize meal (cornmeal)
1 teaspoon garlic salt
¼ teaspoon curry powder
¼ teaspoon mustard powder
2 oz (½ cup) wholemeal flour
2 tablespoons gram (chickpea) flour
4 tablespoons water
1 tablespoon soya sauce

Cut the tofu into ½-inch slices.

Combine the maize meal (cornmeal), garlic salt, curry powder and mustard powder, then spread the mixture out on a plate. Spread the flour out on another plate.

Add the water to the gram flour in a small bowl and mix well with a fork. Stir in the soya sauce.

Dredge each slice of tofu in wholemeal flour, then dip it into the gram flour mixture, and finally dredge it in the maize meal (cornmeal) mixture. Place each slice on a greased baking sheet.

Bake the slices at 375°F (190°C) Gas Mark 5 for about 15 minutes, then turn them over and bake for a further 15 minutes. The ideal accompaniment to this dish is 'Duchesse' All Natural Sandwich Spread, which is a bit like an egg-free tartare sauce (see p. 30). Serve also with cooked vegetables or salad.

Tofu knishes

8 oz (2 cups) wholemeal flour
2 teaspoons baking powder
Pinch sea salt
1 tablespoon soya flour
5 oz ($\frac{2}{3}$ cup) vegetable margarine
4 fl oz ($\frac{1}{2}$ cup) soya milk
4 large or 6-8 small spring onions (scallions)
12 oz ($1\frac{1}{2}$ cups) tofu
4 tablespoons soya yogurt
A little sea salt

Combine the flour, baking powder, salt and soya flour in a large bowl. Cut in 4 oz ($\frac{1}{2}$ cup) margarine then add the soya milk and mix well. Chill the dough for an hour or more.

Chop the spring onions (scallions) finely. Sauté in the remainder of the margarine in a frying pan until beginning to brown.

Put the tofu into a tea towel (dish towel) and squeeze the moisture out of it. Transfer it to a mixing bowl, and stir in the yogurt and a little salt. Add the sautéed spring onions (scallions).

Roll the dough about $\frac{1}{8}$ inch thick on a lightly floured surface. Cut into 3-inch circles. Place about a tablespoon of the tofu mixture on each; fold the dough over and pinch the edges together. Place on a greased baking tin and bake at 350°F (180°C) Gas Mark 4 for about 30 minutes. Serve with salad or cooked vegetables.

Spicy tofu scramble with red pepper and tomato

1 onion
1 large or 2 small cloves garlic
2 tablespoons vegetable margarine
2 red peppers
1 lb tomatoes
$1\frac{1}{4}$-$1\frac{1}{2}$ lb ($2\frac{1}{2}$-3 cups) tofu
2-3 tablespoons soya sauce
1-2 teaspoons tabasco sauce
Buttered wholemeal toast as required

Slice the onion thinly. Chop the garlic finely. Sauté in the margarine for about 3 minutes.

Chop the red peppers finely. Add to the frying pan, lower heat from medium to low, cover pan, and leave to simmer for 3-5 minutes.

Skin and chop the tomatoes. Put the tofu into a tea towel (dish towel) and squeeze the moisture out. Add the tomatoes and tofu to the frying pan, along with the soya sauce and tabasco sauce; raise the heat and stir well until everything is piping hot.

Serve piled on to buttered toast.

Courgette, mushroom and rice savoury

8 oz (1⅓ cups) brown rice
1 onion
1 clove garlic
3 tablespoons vegetable margarine
12 oz courgettes (zucchini)
12 oz mushrooms
2 teaspoons oregano
1 teaspoon basil
1¼ lbs (2½ cups) tofu
4 tablespoons Good-Tasting Yeast* (optional)
Sea salt and freshly ground black pepper

Cook the rice. (This may be done in advance if desired.)

Chop the onion. Crush the garlic. Melt the margarine in a frying pan and sauté the onion and garlic for 3-4 minutes.

Halve or quarter the courgettes (zucchini), depending on size (if they are tiny they may not even need to be halved), then slice them fairly thinly. Chop the mushrooms coarsely. Add the courgettes (zucchini) and mushrooms to the frying pan, along with the oregano and basil, and stir-fry 4-5 minutes.

---

* This is a dried yeast which comes in flakes or powder; it is similar to brewer's yeast but with a milder flavour, and could almost be termed a vegan equivalent to parmesan cheese. It has occasionally been seen in shops here, otherwise it can be ordered direct from the US suppliers. Write to: The Good-Tasting Food Co., PO Box 188, Summertown, TN 38483, USA.

Mash or liquidize the tofu and add to the rice. Stir in the vegetables and half the yeast (if used); season to taste. Turn into a greased casserole, sprinkle with the remainder of the yeast (if used), and bake in a 375°F (190°C) Gas Mark 5 oven for 25-30 minutes until nicely set.

• *Spaghetti with tofu and peas* •

8 oz fresh peas (after shelling) or frozen
3 cloves garlic
2 tablespoons olive oil
2 tablespoons vegetable margarine
1 lb (2 cups) tofu
2 tablespoons soya sauce
12 oz wholemeal spaghetti
3 tablespoons minced parsley
Freshly ground black pepper

Cook the peas until just tender. Drain.

Crush the garlic. Heat the oil and margarine and add the garlic. Cook for a minute or two until the garlic has turned light brown. Mash the tofu and add to the saucepan, along with the soya sauce. Heat gently.

Meanwhile, cook the spaghetti until tender and drain.

Add the peas and parsley to the tofu and heat for a minute or two. Serve the tofu mixture over the spaghetti. Grind black pepper over the top before serving.

Tahu goreng (A Malaysian/Indonesian dish)

1¼ lb (2½ cups) tofu
Cornflour (cornstarch) as required
Vegetable oil for deep-frying
12 oz beansprouts
½ cucumber
2 fresh chillies
3 cloves garlic
3 spring onions (scallions)
2 tablespoons lemon juice
4 tablespoons soya sauce
1 tablespoon raw sugar
Brown rice as required

Dice the tofu. Spread cornflour out on a plate, and roll the tofu cubes in it. Deep-fry the cubes and set aside (keep warm if desired).

Blanch the beansprouts in boiling water for just one minute, then drain and pour cold water over them. Drain well. Slice the cucumber into thin matchsticks.

Chop the chillies, garlic and spring onions (scallions) and put in a liquidizer, along with the lemon juice, soya sauce and sugar. Blend thoroughly.

On a bed of cooked rice, arrange the beansprouts, cucumber and fried tofu cubes. Pour the sauce over this and serve immediately.

Tofu can also be used for a variety of desserts, both simple and elaborate.

• *Pineapple cream* •

1 15-oz tin pineapple in its own juice
12 oz (1½ cups) tofu
2 oz (⅙ cup) honey
1 tablespoon vegetable oil

Put the pineapple into a liquidizer, along with the tofu, the honey, oil, and about a tablespoon of juice from the tin (the rest can be reserved for other purposes). Blend thoroughly. Chill well before serving.

• Gooseberry fool •

12 oz gooseberries
4-5 tablespoons water
4 oz ($\frac{3}{4}$ cup) raw sugar
  (or to taste)

12 oz ($1\frac{1}{2}$ cups) tofu
Pinch sea salt
$\frac{1}{2}$ teaspoon lemon juice
2 tablespoons vegetable oil

Wash, top and tail gooseberries. Put them in a saucepan with the water and sugar, bring to the boil, then lower heat, cover and simmer until tender. Leave to cool.

Put the tofu, salt, lemon juice and oil in a liquidizer, then add the cooked gooseberries. Blend the mixture thoroughly, stirring it between blending, until well mixed.

Serve chilled.

Strawberry 'cheese' dessert

1 lb (2 cups) tofu
6 tablespoons soya yogurt
12 oz fresh strawberries
4 tablespoons raw sugar (or to taste)
1 teaspoon lemon juice

Put the tofu into a tea towel (dish towel) and squeeze as much moisture out as possible. Put the squeezed tofu into a mixing bowl. Stir in the yogurt.

Stir the strawberries into the mixture with a fork, mashing them coarsely as you do so. Finally, stir in the sugar and lemon juice.

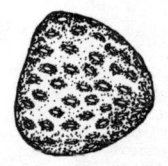

• Rhubarb fool •

1 lb rhubarb
6 tablespoons water
6 oz (1 cup) raw sugar
   (or to taste)
$\frac{1}{2}$ teaspoon powdered
   agar-agar

12 oz (1$\frac{1}{2}$ cups) tofu
Pinch sea salt
$\frac{1}{2}$ teaspoon lemon juice
2 tablespoons vegetable
   oil

Chop the rhubarb into small pieces. Place in a saucepan with the water and about 4 oz ($\frac{3}{4}$ cup) of the sugar. Bring to the boil, then lower heat, cover and simmer until the fruit is well cooked. Sprinkle in the agar agar, raise heat a little and stir. Leave to simmer for a minute longer. Remove from heat and leave to cool briefly.

Put the tofu, salt, lemon juice, oil, and remainder of the sugar in a liquidizer, then add the rhubarb. Blend very thoroughly.

Pour into serving dishes and chill thoroughly.

This next recipe is not really wholefood since fillo pastry is made from white flour. It is very difficult, though, to make really thin pastry from wholemeal flour, and frozen fillo pastry has no additives, so it seemed justifiable to use it here.

• Tofu strudel •

12 oz (1½ cups) tofu
2 tablespoons soya yogurt
2 oz (⅓ cup) raisins
1 teaspoon vanilla essence
3 oz (½ cup) raw sugar

2 tablespoons vegetable margarine
8 sheets frozen fillo pastry*, thawed
Sieved icing sugar or raw sugar ground into a powder as required (optional)

Put the tofu into a clean tea towel (dish towel), and squeeze well to extract as much moisture as possible. Put the tofu into a mixing bowl, and add the yogurt, raisins, vanilla essence and sugar. Mix thoroughly.

Melt the margarine.

Spread a little melted margarine on each sheet of pastry, then ⅛th of the tofu mixture. Roll up the sheet and turn the ends over. Place on an oiled baking sheet.

When all eight sheets have been filled, bake at 425°F

---

* Available at many delicatessens.

(220°C) Gas Mark 7 for 20-30 minutes, until lightly browned.

Sprinkle with icing sugar or finely ground raw sugar if desired, and serve warm if possible.

The calorie-conscious had better skip this next recipe...

• *Hungarian-style layered pancakes* •

5 oz (1¼ cups) 81% flour (or a mixture of 100 per cent wholemeal flour and white flour in preferred proportions)
2 tablespoons soya flour
1 teaspoon baking powder
Pinch sea salt
2 teaspoons vegetable oil + additional as required
4 oz (½ cup) tofu
2 teaspoons raw sugar
1 tablespoon soya yogurt
2 teaspoons lemon juice
Grated rind of ½ lemon
3-4 tablespoons apricot jam
2 oz hazelnuts, almonds or walnuts
2 oz plain chocolate
1 oz creamed coconut
1 tablespoon hot water
Chocolate sauce (optional)

Mix the flour(s), soya flour, baking powder and salt. Add the 2 teaspoons oil, then add a little water at a time, mixing in with a fork until the mixture is the consistency of thick cream. Leave it to stand for half an hour or more. (If it is then too thick a little more water can be added; if too thin a little more flour.)

Mash the tofu. Stir in the sugar, yogurt, lemon juice and lemon rind.

Heat the jam slightly.

Grind the nuts finely. Grate the chocolate. Mix the ground nuts and chocolate together.

Fry the batter for each pancake on both sides in a little oil. Place the first pancake on to an oiled pie dish. Spread a layer of tofu mixture on top. Fry the next pancake; top with a layer of apricot jam. Fry a third pancake and spread some of the nut and chocolate mixture on top. Continue layering until all the ingredients have been used, finishing up with a pancake on top.

Grate or finely chop the coconut and mix with the hot water. Spread over the top pancake. Bake at 375°F (190°C) Gas Mark 5 for 15-20 minutes.

Slice into 4 servings, like cake and serve hot. Chocolate sauce may seem like gilding the lily, but if you are going to make a dessert like this then why not? (NB The simplest sauce I know – unless you buy a bottled one – is to heat Cadbury's Chocolate Spread with a little water.)

· Ice-cream ·

The most important thing to remember about homemade ice creams is that it is never enough just to make up the mixture and put it in the freezer, for it will invariably crystallize. With the freezer on its coldest setting it will normally take about 2-3 hours for the mixture to freeze. After the first half-hour it should be well mixed, and then every 20 minutes or so after that. There is usually an optimum point when the mixture is frozen but still creamy; if it is not possible to serve it at that moment and it freezes rather hard afterwards, then it is a good idea to keep it in the fridge for 10-15 minutes before serving. One final tip: if in spite of all efforts the ice cream still ends up brick hard, and you have a powerful liquidizer or a food processor, the best thing is to chop up the 'bricks,' blend thoroughly and dish up immediately as 'soft-serve' ice cream.

Maple walnut tofu ice cream

2 oz ($\frac{1}{3}$ cup) tofu
$\frac{1}{4}$ pint ($\frac{2}{3}$ cup) soya milk
1 oz ($\frac{1}{8}$ cup) soft vegetable margarine
$\frac{1}{4}$ pint ($\frac{2}{3}$ cup) maple syrup
1 teaspoon vanilla essence
2 teaspoons lemon juice
Pinch sea salt
2 oz ($\frac{1}{2}$ cup) walnut pieces

Put the tofu, soya milk, margarine, maple syrup, vanilla essence, lemon juice and salt in the liquidizer and blend thoroughly.

Stir in the walnut pieces (if they are large ones then break or chop them into small pieces).

Place the mixture in a container in the freezer and stir frequently as per the instructions above.

• Raspberry tofu ice cream •

8 oz (1 cup) tofu
4 tablespoons soya milk
2 oz ($\frac{1}{3}$ cup) raw sugar
2 tablespoons vegetable oil
Pinch sea salt

8 oz fresh raspberries
1 teaspoon lemon juice
$\frac{1}{2}$ teaspoon vanilla essence
$\frac{1}{8}$ teaspoon almond essence

Put the tofu, soya milk, sugar, oil and salt in the liquidizer and blend thoroughly.

Put the raspberries through a sieve. Discard the seeds and put the purée into the liquidizer along with the lemon juice, vanilla and almond essences. Blend thoroughly.

Follow the instructions above for freezing the ice cream.

The use of tofu need not be confined to savoury dishes and desserts, it can be used in many other ways as well. In the recipe below it is used as a substitute for eggs and milk to make a cholesterol-free version of a popular American breakfast dish.

• *Tofu French toast* •

12 oz (1½ cups) soft or medium tofu
8 fl oz (1 cup) water
4 tablespoons vegetable oil
Pinch sea salt
1 teaspoon vanilla essence
3-4 teaspoons raw sugar
Approximately 8 slices wholemeal bread
Margarine as required for frying

Put the tofu, water, oil, salt, vanilla and sugar in a liquidizer and blend thoroughly. Pour the mixture into a shallow bowl, and dip the slices of bread in it.

Heat a little margarine in a frying pan, and fry the bread over a moderate heat until browned on both sides.

Serve with maple syrup, or a mixture of raw sugar and cinnamon, or raw sugar jam.

At tea-time tofu can be used to make deliciously light scones.

Queen scones

9 oz (2¼ cups) wholemeal flour
2 teaspoons baking powder
Pinch sea salt
1½ oz (¼ cup) raw sugar
2 fl oz (¼ cup) vegetable oil
3 oz (½ cup) sultanas
4 oz (½ cup) medium or soft tofu
4 fl oz (½ cup) water

Combine the flour, baking powder, salt and sugar in a bowl. Mix well. Stir in the oil and then the sultanas.

Put the tofu and water in a liquidizer and blend well. Pour into the dry mixture and stir well.

Turn out on to a floured board, roll the dough out and cut it into scones. Place the scones on an oiled baking sheet and bake at 425°F (220°C) Gas Mark 7 for 15 minutes.

(Makes 16 scones.)

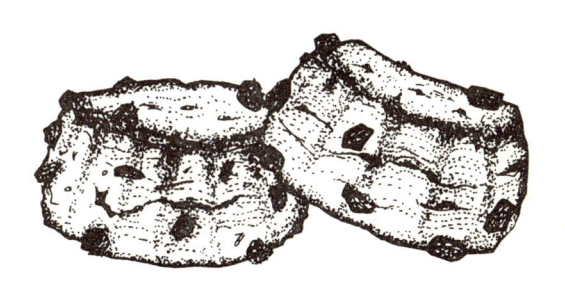

· 2 ·
Frozen and dried-frozen tofu

One of the first questions any freezer owner will ask is whether tofu can be frozen. The answer is yes, but do not expect it to be the same product when it is defrosted. The nutritional content remains as high, but the texture changes quite radically, becoming rather spongy and chewy, and therefore requiring a new set of recipes.

When freezing tofu it is best to cut it up into chunks of 2-3 oz rather than freezing a whole block at a time, in order to facilitate defrosting. If you have a small amount left over from a block of tofu you can freeze that, and then later add other leftover chunks until there is sufficient to defrost and use in a dish.

Frozen tofu is also sold in dried form. (No, it's not freeze-dried; that is a completely different process.) Dried tofu certainly is a useful product to have in the larder for emergencies, but I must admit that I find home-frozen tofu much nicer. For dishes where the tofu is crumbled into a 'mince', one really does need to use frozen rather than dried tofu.

The best way to defrost frozen tofu – and the only way to rehydrate dried tofu – is to pour boiling water over it for about 10-15 minutes before draining it. The most important step to remember is to *squeeze* it, gently but thoroughly, after draining and before using it in a dish. If you don't the end result is likely to be soggy and unappetizing.

Lentil tofu with macaroni

1 lb frozen or 4 oz dried tofu
2 onions
2 tablespoons vegetable oil
1 clove garlic
1½ pints (3¾ cups) water
1 tablespoon yeast extract
2 teaspoons basil
2 teaspoons oregano
Freshly ground black pepper
4 oz (¾ cup) red lentils
10 oz (2½ cups) wholemeal macaroni

Defrost the frozen tofu or rehydrate the dried tofu. Squeeze well. Cut into cubes.

Chop the onions. Sauté in the oil until beginning to brown. Chop the garlic finely and add to the saucepan. Cook for another minute or two, then add the tofu cubes and stir for a further 2 minutes.

Add the water, yeast extract, herbs and pepper. Bring to the boil, then lower heat, cover saucepan, and simmer for 15-20 minutes.

Add the lentils to the saucepan and cook for a further 15-20 minutes.

Serve over the cooked macaroni.

Tofu and green pepper dish

2 lb frozen or 8 oz
  dried tofu
1 pint (2½ cups) water
8 tablespoons soya sauce
2 teaspoons grated fresh
  ginger
2 cloves garlic
Cornflour (cornstarch)
  as required

Oil for deep-frying
1 onion
2 green peppers
2 tablespoons vegetable
  margarine
8 oz tomatoes
1 teaspoon honey

Reconstitute the tofu, cool and squeeze out excess liquid.

Bring to the boil in a saucepan 2 cups water, 6 tablespoons soya sauce, the ginger, and one clove of garlic, crushed. Slice the tofu into ½ inch strips and place them in the saucepan. Lower heat, and simmer for about 15 minutes. Cool slightly, then squeeze excess moisture from the strips and roll them lightly in cornflour (cornstarch). (This part may all be done in advance if desired.)

Deep-fry the tofu strips until browned and crispy. Set aside.

Chop the onion and slice the green pepper thinly and sauté both in the margarine for 2-3 minutes. Crush the second clove of garlic and add it to the saucepan; cook for a further minute or two. Peel the tomatoes, chop them and add to the saucepan. Cook for a further 2-3 minutes.

Then add the remaining water, remaining 2 tablespoons soya sauce, and honey; bring to the boil. Add the tofu strips to the sauce, mix them in very thoroughly, then lower heat, cover and simmer for about 10 minutes.

Serve immediately, with boiled, baked or mashed potatoes if desired (but only for those with a large appetite – it is a very filling dish).

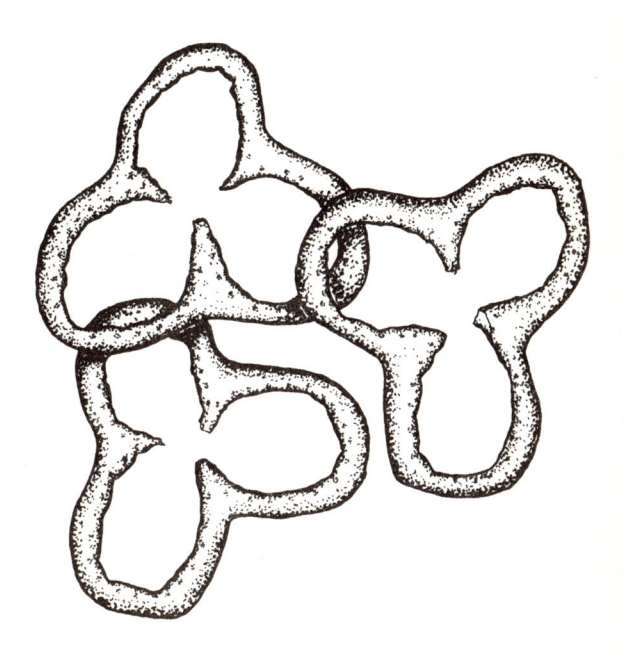

Peking noodles

1 lb (2 cups) frozen
  tofu
2 teaspoons yeast extract
$\frac{1}{4}$ pint ($\frac{2}{3}$ cup) + 6
  tablespoons water
4 spring onions
  (scallions)
$\frac{1}{2}$ cucumber
8 oz mung bean sprouts
2 cloves garlic
2 tablespoons vegetable
  oil
3 tablespoons Hoisin
  sauce*
2 teaspoons soya sauce
1 tablespoon cider
  vinegar
12 oz Chinese noodles

Defrost the tofu. Squeeze well. Dissolve the yeast extract in the $\frac{1}{4}$ pint water. Crumble the tofu into this, and simmer for a minute or two (the liquid should be completely absorbed). Set aside.

Mince two of the spring onions (scallions). Coarsely grate the cucumber. Mix these ingredients together with the bean sprouts, and set aside.

Chop the garlic finely. Add to the oil in a wok and stir in the tofu. Stir-fry for a minute or two.

Mince the other two spring onions (scallions) and add them to the wok, along with the Hoisin sauce, soya sauce, vinegar, and 6 tablespoons water. Simmer this mixture briefly while cooking the noodles until just tender, according to the instructions on the packet.

Serve the noodles with the tofu sauce poured over them, topped with the mixture of bean sprouts, cucumber and spring onions (scallions).

* Available at Chinese shops.

• Swiss steak •

$1\frac{1}{4}$ lb ($2\frac{1}{2}$ cups) frozen tofu
2 teaspoons yeast extract
$\frac{1}{2}$ pint ($1\frac{1}{3}$ cup) + 2 tablespoons water
2 oz ($\frac{1}{2}$ cup) + 2 tablespoons wholemeal flour
1 teaspoon paprika
1 teaspoon oregano
1 teaspoon freshly ground black pepper (+ additional to taste)
4 tablespoons vegetable oil
2 onions
8 oz tomatoes
2 sticks celery
1 green pepper
4 oz mushrooms

For this dish it is easiest if the tofu has been frozen in slices $\frac{1}{3}$-$\frac{1}{2}$ inch thick. Defrost the slices and squeeze excess liquid from them. Dissolve the yeast extract in $\frac{1}{2}$ pint ($1\frac{1}{3}$ cups) warm water. Place the tofu slices in a shallow bowl, and pour the yeast extract liquid over them. Leave to marinate for an hour or two, turning the slices occasionally if possible.

Combine the 2 oz ($\frac{1}{2}$ cup) flour with the paprika, oregano, and teaspoon pepper and spread out on a plate. Lift each tofu slice from the marinade, gently squeezing the marinade from it back into the bowl, and coat both sides with the flour. Sauté in 2 tablespoons of the vegetable oil in a frying pan, turning once, until lightly browned on both sides. Set aside.

Chop the onions and sauté in the remaining oil for 2-3 minutes. Peel and chop the tomatoes. Chop the celery, green pepper and mushrooms finely. Add to the saucepan.

Add the yeast extract marinade to the saucepan, bring to the boil, cover and simmer for about 3 minutes.

Combine the 2 tablespoons flour with the 2 tablespoons water in a cup. Stir this into the vegetable mixture until thickened.

Place the tofu slices at the bottom of an oiled casserole. Pour the vegetable mixture over them. Bake at 350°F (180°C) Gas Mark 4 for about half an hour. Nice with baked or sauté potatoes.

• Spicey ricey casserole •

8 oz (1⅓ cup) brown rice
1 lb (2 cups) frozen tofu
¼ pint (⅔ cup) water
2 teaspoons yeast extract
2 onions
2 tablespoons vegetable oil
1 large green pepper
4 sticks celery
1 clove garlic
2 fresh chillies
2 tablespoons vegetable margarine
2 tablespoons wholemeal flour
2 teaspoons curry powder
½ pint (1⅓ cups) soya milk
1 15-oz tin tomatoes
2 oz (½ cup) coarsely chopped walnuts
Good-Tasting Yeast (see p. 37) as required (optional)

Cook the rice until tender. Set aside.

Defrost the tofu, squeeze well to extract as much moisture as possible. Bring the water to the boil, dissolve the yeast extract in it, and crumble the tofu into the saucepan. Lower heat and simmer for a minute or so until all the liquid has been absorbed. Set aside.

Chop the onions and sauté in the oil for 2-3 minutes. Chop the green pepper, celery, garlic and chillies and add to the onion; cook for a few minutes longer, stirring occasionally. Add the tofu and continue stir-frying for 2-3 minutes longer.

Melt the margarine in a separate saucepan and add the flour and the curry powder, then slowly pour in the soya milk, stirring constantly to avoid lumps, and bring to the boil.

Empty the contents of the tin of tomatoes into a liquidizer and blend thoroughly.

In a large mixing bowl combine the rice, vegetable and tofu mixture, curry sauce, puréed tomatoes, and walnuts. Turn the mixture into a large oiled casserole, sprinkle with Good-Tasting Yeast if using, and bake at 375°F (190°C) Gas Mark 5 for 25-30 minutes.

• Savoury tofu 'mince' •

1 lb (2 cups) frozen tofu
1 large onion
3 sticks celery
2 carrots
¾ pint (2 cups) water

2-3 teaspoons yeast extract
3-4 teaspoons curry powder
1 oz ($\frac{1}{6}$ cup) raisins

Defrost the tofu and squeeze out as much moisture as possible.

Chop the onion, celery and carrots finely. Place in a saucepan. Crumble the tofu into the saucepan. Add the water and bring to the boil. Stir in the yeast extract, curry powder and raisins. Lower heat and simmer for about 15 minutes.

Serve with brown rice, pasta or mashed potatoes.

• Oaty tofu and bean crumble •

8 oz (1 cup) haricot (navy) beans
1 lb (2 cups) frozen tofu
¼ pint (⅔ cup) water
2-3 teaspoons yeast extract
2 onions
3 cloves garlic
4 fl oz (½ cup) vegetable oil
1 lb tomatoes
1 teaspoon ground cumin
2 teaspoons dried basil
4-5 oz cabbage
2 tablespoons soya sauce
8 oz (2 cups) rolled oats
4 oz (1 cup) wholemeal flour
2 oz (4 tablespoons) peanuts
1 oz (2 tablespoons) sesame seeds

Soak the beans overnight, then cook until tender.

Defrost the tofu. Heat the water and dissolve the yeast extract in it. Crumble the drained and squeezed tofu into the saucepan and cook for 2-3 minutes until the liquid has been absorbed.

Chop the onions and garlic finely. Sauté in 1 oz of the oil until beginning to brown. Add the tofu and cook for a further 2-3 minutes.

Chop the tomatoes and add them to the saucepan, along with the cumin, basil, and the drained cooked beans. Stir well, then cook uncovered for 6 or 7 minutes.

Shred the cabbage and add it to the saucepan along with the soya sauce. Cover the pan and cook for a further 2-3 minutes.

Meanwhile, combine the oats, flour, peanuts and sesame seeds in a mixing bowl, and stir in the remaining oil.

Turn the bean and tofu mixture into an oiled casserole and top with the oat mixture. Bake at 375°F (190°C) Gas Mark 5 for about 30 minutes until brown.

· Tofu goulash ·

5 oz *dried-frozen tofu*
2 *onions*
1 *large or 2 small green peppers*
3 *tablespoons vegetable oil*
2 *tablespoons flour plus additional for coating*
3 *teaspoons paprika*
8 oz *tomatoes*
1 *pint (2½ cups) water*
3 *teaspoons yeast extract*
3 *tablespoons tomato purée (paste)*
Freshly ground black pepper to taste
Wholemeal noodles as required

Rehydrate the tofu.

Chop the onions and green pepper. Sauté in the oil for 3-4 minutes.

Squeeze excess liquid from the tofu and cut into cubes approximately 1 inch by 1 inch by $\frac{1}{2}$ inch. Spread some wholemeal flour on to a plate and roll the cubes in this. Add to the saucepan and stir well for about 2 minutes.

Sprinkle in the paprika and the flour and stir for another 2 minutes.

Chop the tomatoes coarsely (skinned if desired). Add them to the saucepan along with the water, yeast extract, tomato purée (paste), and pepper. Bring to the boil, lower heat, cover saucepan and simmer for about 15 minutes, stirring occasionally. Serve over cooked noodles.

Frozen tofu can be used for Oriental dishes, as a shortcut in making 'Spiced pressed tofu', traditionally a long and delicate process.

• *Spiced pressed tofu* •

1-1¼ lb (2-2½ cups) frozen tofu
2 large cloves garlic
2 tablespoons raw sugar
2 teaspoons vegetable oil
4 tablespoons soya sauce
1 teaspoon five-spice powder (available at Oriental food shops)

Defrost the tofu, squeeze it to remove the liquid, and cut it into thin strips.

Crush the garlic. Put it into a saucepan along with the sugar, oil, soya sauce and five-spice powder, and heat it gently for about 2-3 minutes.

Add the tofu strips and cook for a further 2-3 minutes. Remove from heat and either use immediately or cool and then refrigerate for up to two weeks.

Carrots and celery with spiced pressed tofu

8 oz carrots
6 sticks celery
3 tablespoons vegetable oil
1-1¼ lb (2-2½ cups) spiced pressed tofu
1½ tablespoons cider vinegar
1 tablespoon sesame oil
Brown rice as required

Slice the carrots into matchsticks. Slice the celery similarly.

Heat the vegetable oil in a wok or frying pan and stir-fry the carrots and celery for 3-4 minutes, until crisp-tender.

Add the spiced pressed tofu and heat thoroughly. Sprinkle in the vinegar and sesame oil, and serve immediately over brown rice.

Cabbage with spiced pressed tofu

1 lb (2 cups) spiced
 pressed tofu
1¼ lb cabbage
1 teaspoon sea salt
2 tablespoons sesame oil

1 teaspoon raw sugar
4 tablespoons soya sauce
Pinch of five-spice
 powder
Brown rice as required

Cut the tofu into small cubes. Set aside.

Shred the cabbage coarsely. Bring a saucepan of water to the boil, sprinkle in the salt, then plunge the cabbage into the water and cook for 2 minutes. Drain thoroughly.

Combine the sesame oil, sugar, soya sauce and five-spice powder in a wok or frying pan. Add the cabbage and mix thoroughly over a gentle heat. Finally, stir in the spiced pressed tofu cubes and serve immediately over brown rice.

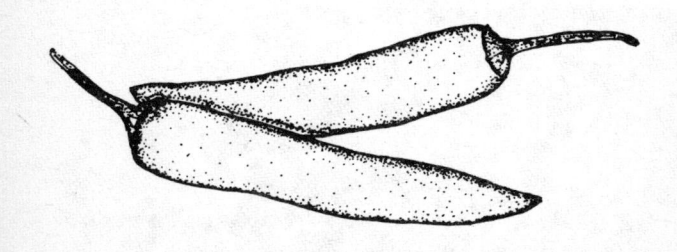

Cabbage and Chinese mushrooms with spiced pressed tofu

6-8 dried Chinese mushrooms (about 1 oz)
1-2 fresh chillies
2-3 spring onions (scallions)
2 cloves garlic
2 tablespoons vegetable oil
2 teaspoons finely minced fresh ginger
8 oz cabbage
1 tablespoon cider vinegar
1 tablespoon soya sauce
2 teaspoons sesame oil
1 lb (2 cups) spiced pressed tofu
Brown rice as required

Cover the dried mushrooms with hot water and leave to soak for about half an hour.

Mince the chillies finely (making certain all seeds are removed), and the spring onions (scallions). Drain and chop the mushrooms, discarding the stalks. Set aside.

Crush the garlic. Heat the vegetable oil in a wok and add the finely minced ginger and the crushed garlic. Stir-fry for 30-45 seconds until very lightly browned. Add the spring onions (scallions), chillies and mushrooms. Stir-fry for a further 30 seconds.

Chop the cabbage and add to the wok. Stir-fry for a minute or two. Add the vinegar, then the soya sauce and sesame oil, and finally the strips of pressed tofu. Continue stir-frying briefly until the cabbage is completely wilted, and serve immediately over brown rice.

· 3 ·
Smoked tofu

At time of writing, smoked tofu is produced by only one manufacturer in the UK (Cauldron Foods, 4 Conduit Place, Lower Ashley Road, St Paul's, Bristol), but it is widely available at health food stores here and in the USA and has been such a great success that I have felt no hesitation about including it in this book. It might not be ideal for those on a low-sodium diet, but, with a slightly lower fat content, higher protein content, and identical calorie content to regular tofu, it can be recommended as a highly nutritious food.

The texture of smoked tofu is more solid than firm tofu and is similar to processed dairy cheese. Indeed, it is very pleasant sliced and eaten raw in a sandwich. When fried or grilled it obtains a nice brown crispiness. Vegetarians who used to enjoy ham or bacon will certainly welcome this product: it is not an 'imitation' of anything, but it satisfies the taste for a savoury smoked food.

Smoked tofu

Smoked tofu makes a wonderful addition to soups.

• *Lentil and smoked tofu soup* •

6 oz smoked tofu
2 cloves garlic
1½ pints (4 cups) water
4 oz (¾ cup) red lentils
2 cloves
2 tablespoons minced parsley
12 oz potatoes
Freshly ground black pepper

Dice the tofu finely. Crush the garlic. Put the water, lentils, tofu, garlic, cloves, and parsley in a saucepan and bring to the boil.

Scrape or peel the potatoes and dice them very finely. Add them to the saucepan. Lower heat, cover saucepan, and simmer for about 20 minutes, by which time both lentils and potatoes should be very soft. Add pepper to taste (salt should not be necessary). Serve immediately.

The following recipe is too solid to be called a soup but not really substantial enough to be called a stew or casserole. Anyway, it makes a pleasant lunch dish.

• Winter hodge podge •

8 oz carrots
8 oz turnips
2 onions
3 sticks celery
2 leeks
4 oz smoked tofu
2 tablespoons vegetable oil
1½ pints vegetable stock or water

1 teaspoon dried mixed herbs
4 oz macaroni
8 oz cabbage
Sea salt and freshly ground black pepper
2 tablespoons minced parsley

Peel and chop the carrots, turnips and onions. Clean and chop the celery and leeks. Dice the tofu finely. Sauté all these ingredients in the oil for about 5 minutes.

Add the stock or water and herbs, bring to the boil, then lower heat, cover and simmer for about 20 minutes.

Add the macaroni to the saucepan and cook for a further 10 minutes.

Shred the cabbage and add it to the saucepan. Simmer for a final 5 minutes. Adjust seasoning.

Serve immediately, sprinkled with parsley, with wholemeal bread.

a bit 'wholesome'
try Cranks Goulash

Smoked tofu

One of the most traditional of all-American sandwiches is the BLT – Bacon, Lettuce, and Tomato – and everyone can now enjoy something remarkably similar without using any animal products at all. I have not given specific amounts to be used below, as that is very much a matter of the size of the loaf of bread and personal preference.

• *Smoked tofu, lettuce and tomato* • *sandwich*

Smoked tofu
Vegetable oil
Slices of wholemeal bread
Vegetable margarine
'Duchesse' Tofu Dressing and Dip (or homemade tofu mayonnaise)
Tomatoes
Lettuce

Slice the smoked tofu as thinly as possible, and fry the slices in a little oil until browned on both sides.

Toast the bread. Spread every slice with margarine and alternate slices with tofu mayonnaise as well.

Slice the tomatoes as thinly as possible.

On the slices of toast which have been spread with tofu mayonnaise place the fried slices of smoked tofu, the thinly sliced tomatoes, and lots of lettuce (American sandwiches always bulge at the seams). Serve immediately.

Smoked tofu can be used in a variety of simple recipes.

· *Smoked tofu fritters* ·

12 oz smoked tofu
8 tablespoons vegetable oil
8 oz (2 cups) wholemeal flour
1½ teaspoons baking powder
Pinch sea salt
6-8 tablespoons soya milk
4 tomatoes

Chop the smoked tofu into tiny cubes. Fry in half the oil in a frying pan until lightly browned. Remove the cubes from the frying pan, draining them on kitchen (paper) towels, but leave the remainder of the oil in the frying pan.

In a small saucepan heat the other half of the oil and stir in the flour. Remove from the heat and stir in the baking powder and salt, then pour in enough soya milk to make a thick cream. Finally, stir in the cubes of smoked tofu.

Drop the fritter mixture by tablespoonfuls into the remaining oil in the frying pan. Slice the tomatoes thinly and fry them at the same time. Serve immediately.

Central American-style smokey pasta and bean dish

10 oz wholemeal macaroni or other pasta shapes
8 oz smoked tofu
4 cloves garlic
2 tablespoons vegetable oil
2 15-oz tins red kidney beans
1 tablespoon ground cumin
Freshly ground black pepper to taste

Cook the pasta in lightly salted boiling water until tender.

Meanwhile, dice the smoked tofu finely. Chop the garlic very finely. Fry in the oil in a frying pan over medium heat until both the tofu and garlic are lightly browned.

Drain the beans, retaining about 2 tablespoons of the liquid.

When the pasta is cooked drain it well. Put it back in the saucepan, along with the tofu and garlic, beans, bean liquid, cumin and pepper (additional salt should not be necessary). Mix well, then cook for a further 4-5 minutes over minimum heat. Serve immediately, accompanied by a side salad.

Smokey bean fritters

8 oz smoked tofu
2 14-oz tins chick peas
   (garbanzo beans)
1 onion
Freshly ground black
   pepper
Vegetable oil for frying

Put the tofu, drained chick peas (garbanzo beans) and onion through a mincer/grinder.

Add pepper to taste (salt should not be required). Transfer to a mixing bowl and mix well, then form into patties with your hands.

Shallow-fry in oil until lightly browned on both sides. Serve immediately, with gravy or sauce and cooked vegetables.

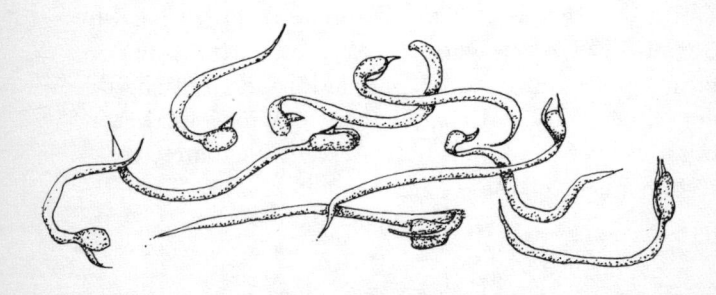

• Smoked tofu pasties •

6 8 oz smoked tofu
6 8 oz tomatoes
1 3 onions
1 teaspoon mixed herbs

Sea salt and freshly
ground black pepper
12 oz wholemeal pastry
10oz

Chop the smoked tofu into small cubes. Peel and chop the tomatoes. Peel and chop the onions. Mix together in a bowl, along with the herbs, and salt and pepper to taste.

Divide the pastry into 8 portions. Roll each one out, and spoon some of the tofu mixture on to half; fold over and place on a baking sheet. When all the pasties have been filled and folded, score the tops lightly with a knife or prick them with a fork. Bake at 425°F (220°C) Gas Mark 7 for 20 minutes, then lower heat and bake for a further half-hour at 350°F (180°C) Gas Mark 4. Serve with cooked vegetables or salad.

• *Steamed savoury smoked tofu pudding* •

8 oz (2 cups) wholemeal flour
3 teaspoons baking powder
1 teaspoon sea salt
4 oz ($\frac{1}{2}$ cup) hard vegetable fat (e.g. Pura)

8 oz smoked tofu
2 onions
1 small (8-oz) tin tomatoes
1 teaspoon sage
Tomato sauce as required

Mix the flour, baking powder and salt in a large bowl. Grate the fat and mix it in. Add enough water to make a dough, and roll out about two-thirds of it, then transfer it to a large greased pudding bowl.

Dice the smoked tofu. Chop the onions. Remove the tomatoes from the tin (the juice can be kept for the sauce if desired) and chop them coarsely. Combine these ingredients in a bowl and stir in the sage. Spoon this mixture into the pastry-lined pudding bowl.

Roll out the remaining third of pastry to make a lid and fit it over the tofu mixture. Cover the bowl with tin foil, and place in a large saucepan of boiling water. Lower heat and leave it to steam for about 2 hours.

Serve the pudding with tomato sauce – a good quality proprietary brand or homemade (the quickest home-made sauce is simply a tin of tomatoes liquidized with herbs and seasonings to taste). Accompany with vegetables.

Smoked tofu charlotte

8 oz mushrooms
5 sticks celery
2½ oz (¼ cup + 1 tablespoon) vegetable margarine
6 oz smoked tofu
2 tablespoons vegetable oil
2 oz (½ cup) wholemeal flour
¾ pint (2 cups) soya milk
Sea salt and freshly ground black pepper
4 oz (2 cups) wholemeal breadcrumbs

Chop the mushrooms and celery. Sauté them in 2 oz (¼ cup) margarine for a few minutes.

Dice the smoked tofu and sauté in the oil in a frying pan at the same time.

Stir the flour into the mushrooms and celery, cook for about a minute, then gradually stir in the soya milk. Stir until thickened, then season. Stir in the tofu.

Transfer to a greased baking dish and top with breadcrumbs. Sprinkle shavings of the remaining margarine on top, and bake at 375°F (190°C) Gas Mark 5 for 15-20 minutes. Serve immediately, accompanied by baked potatoes.

• Leek and smoked tofu au gratin •

6 oz (¾ cup) vegetable margarine
3 oz (¾ cup) soya flour
2 teaspoons yeast extract
8 medium-sized leeks
8 oz smoked tofu
2 tablespoons vegetable oil
1½ oz (⅓ cup) wholemeal flour
1 pint (2½ cups) soya milk
Sea salt and freshly ground black pepper
2 oz (1 cup) fresh breadcrumbs

Make the 'cheese' by melting 4 oz (½ cup) of the margarine and stirring in the soya flour and yeast extract. Spread out on a plate and place in the fridge to cool.

Trim and wash the leeks and chop them coarsely. Cook in a small amount of lightly salted boiling water until tender. Drain.

Meanwhile, dice the tofu and sauté in the oil until lightly browned.

Melt the remainder of the margarine in a saucepan and stir in the flour. Cook for a minute and then gradually stir in the soya milk to make a white sauce. Bring to the boil, stirring constantly. Then stir in about three-quarters of the 'cheese'. Taste and add additional seasoning if required.

Place the cooked leeks and sautéed tofu in a shallow ovenproof dish and pour the sauce over them. Top with the breadcrumbs and the remainder of the 'cheese', finely chopped or grated. Place under a moderate grill (broiler) until nicely browned. Serve immediately.

• Smoked tofu and mashed potato cakes •

1 lb potatoes
1 lb smoked tofu
2 tablespoons finely chopped parsley
1-2 tablespoons grated onion
Freshly ground black pepper to taste
Wholemeal flour as required
Vegetable oil for frying

Cook the potatoes until tender, then cool, peel and mash.

Put the tofu through a mincer.

Combine the mashed potato, tofu, parsley, onion and pepper, and form into patties. Dip them lightly, on both sides, in the flour.

Shallow-fry the cakes on both sides until nicely browned. Serve immediately, with salad or cooked seasonal vegetables.

Smoked tofu can also be used in Continental-style dishes as in the recipes below.

• Risi e bisi •

12 oz (2 cups) brown rice
2 teaspoons yeast extract
6 oz smoked tofu
2 tablespoons vegetable margarine
2 tablespoons olive oil
1 oz parsley
2 sticks celery
1 lb frozen peas
4 tablespoons cider vinegar
Freshly ground black pepper and salt
3 tablespoons Good-Tasting Yeast (see p. 37) (optional)

Cover the rice with boiling water and leave to soak for several hours. Drain the rice, then cover it with water by about $\frac{1}{2}$ inch, and bring to the boil. When the water is boiling stir in the yeast extract. Lower the heat, cover the saucepan, and leave to simmer until tender (about 25 minutes).

Cut the smoked tofu into small cubes. Sauté them in the margarine and the olive oil for about 5 minutes.

Chop the parsley and celery, add them to the smoked tofu, and cook for a further 3-4 minutes. Add the peas and vinegar, stir well, raise the heat for 2-3 minutes, then cover the saucepan and lower the heat and cook for a few minutes until just tender.

Stir this mixture into the cooked rice and leave for a minute or two longer. Finally, stir in the seasonings and the yeast (if used). Serve immediately.

• *Spaghetti milanese* •

1 onion
4 oz mushrooms
1½ oz (3 tablespoons) vegetable margarine
Grating of fresh nutmeg
⅛ teaspoon thyme
Freshly ground black pepper
½ teaspoon raw sugar
1 15-oz tin tomatoes
8 oz smoked tofu
12 oz wholemeal spaghetti
Good-Tasting Yeast (see p. 37) (optional)

Chop the onion and mushrooms and cook in 1 oz (2 tablespoons) margarine for 3-5 minutes.

Add the herbs and seasonings and the tin of tomatoes and stir well. Bring to the boil, lower heat and simmer for about 15 minutes.

Chop the smoked tofu into small dice and add to the saucepan. Cook for a further 5 minutes.

Meanwhile, cook the spaghetti until tender and toss with the remainder of the margarine.

Serve the spaghetti with the sauce poured over it, sprinkled with the yeast if desired.

• *Part Three* •

TEMPEH

TEMPEH

Pronounced 'tempay' (with the accent on the first syllable), this soya food originated in Indonesia. Cooked soya beans are bound together by spores which cause them to ferment and join together into a solid mass. Tempeh is high in protein, low in fat, and cholesterol free. Unlike tofu, it has a high fibre content, and because of the fermentation process the fibre is easily digested. Another extremely valuable property of tempeh is that it is one of the few plant foods containing naturally occurring vitamin B12; vegans who eat tempeh regularly should not need to take supplements or seek foods with added B12.

Tempeh is very versatile. It can be steamed, grilled, sautéed or deep-fried. When fried it acquires a chewiness which will be appreciated by those who like to get their teeth into something with a 'bite'. Unlike tofu, tempeh does have a distinct flavour of its own, which becomes stronger the longer it is fermented. This is evidenced by the amount of black patches (which are similar in nature to the patches in blue cheeses), so if trying tempeh for the first time, or serving it to someone unfamiliar with it, it is best to choose a light-coloured block.

Tempeh is not a high-technology product and could be made at home. The difficulty is that in order to ferment properly it requires a steady temperature of around 90°F, not easy to maintain in Britain. Of course there are ways of doing it – a light bulb rigged up inside a box is one suggestion I've been given – but not being any good at DIY, I've not tried it and do not like passing on instructions for something I cannot vouch for. Also, a tempeh manufacturer advised me it took her many months of trial and error before she got it right, so I recommend purchasing rather than making it at home.

Tempeh Foods (Unit 1, Cowslip Farm, Witnesham, Ipswich, Suffolk) distribute tempeh to a number of health food stores in England. There are also some individual wholefood shops who make their own tempeh, so it is worth asking around. In Scotland tempeh is available at Real Foods (37 Broughton Street, Edinburgh). It is widely available in the USA.

The main problem with tempeh is that it is a 'live' food which, if not frozen, will continue fermenting. Fortunately, because of the proliferation of frozen wholefood convenience meals, more and more health food stores are acquiring freezers, which should help to facilitate the wider distribution of tempeh.

Tempeh will keep in a freezer for three months. In a fridge it will keep for three or four days, though the flavour will grow stronger during that period. Tempeh should be thawed before using it; this will take roughly 2 to 3 hours at room temperature and about 12 hours in the refrigerator. It should never be eaten raw.

Instructions about the amount of time needed to steam tempeh range from 5 minutes to half an hour; 15-20 minutes seems about right to me, but it is clearly not necessary to follow a hard and fast rule. A steamer can be used so that the tempeh is not actually in the water. (I improvise one by putting the lid of a small saucepan inside a larger pan containing a little simmering water, putting the tempeh on top, and covering the pan.) Alternatively, the tempeh can be cooked directly in the water or other liquid, a method which is particularly useful if one wants it to absorb flavours from the liquid, but the pan must then be closely watched to make certain the liquid does not evaporate, leaving the tempeh to burn.

Spaghetti with tempeh sauce

2 onions
1-2 cloves garlic
2 tablespoons olive oil
2 sticks celery
4 oz mushrooms
1 15-oz tin tomatoes
4 tablespoons tomato
   purée (paste)
$\frac{1}{4}$ pint ($\frac{2}{3}$ cup) water
3 teaspoons dried basil
2 teaspoons dried
   marjoram
Sea salt and freshly
   ground black pepper
8 oz tempeh
12 oz wholemeal
   spaghetti

Chop the onions. Mince the garlic. Sauté in the oil for 2-3 minutes.

Chop the celery and mushrooms and add them to the saucepan. Stir well and cook for a further 2-3 minutes.

Add the tomatoes (mashing them with a spoon while doing so), tomato purée, water, herbs and seasoning. Crumble the tempeh into the saucepan. Stir well. Bring to the boil, then lower heat and simmer for about 20 minutes, stirring occasionally while the spaghetti is cooking.

When the spaghetti is ready, drain it well, then pour the sauce over it.

There are basically two ways of stuffing green peppers. One is to slice off the top and fill the whole pepper. The other is to halve the pepper and fill each half. My own preference is for the latter method, because the filling can be piled up high if the pepper isn't quite big enough, but either method is fine for the recipe below.

• *Tempeh stuffed peppers* •

4 large or 8 small green peppers
1 lb tempeh
1 onion
2 tablespoons vegetable oil
2 sticks celery
1 carrot
1 tablespoon tomato purée (paste)
2 tablespoons soya sauce
2 teaspoons dried marjoram
2 oz (1 cup) fresh wholemeal breadcrumbs
Vegetable margarine as required

Parboil the peppers for 3-4 minutes. Drain and cool.

Steam the tempeh for about 15 minutes (see pp. 86-7).

Chop the onion finely and sauté for 3-4 minutes in the oil, until just beginning to brown. Chop the celery finely. Grate the carrot.

Mash the tempeh in a bowl. Add the onion, celery, carrot, tomato purée (paste), soya sauce and marjoram. Mix well.

Slice the tops off the green peppers or slice them in half (see note above), remove the seeds, place them on a greased baking sheet and fill them with the tempeh mixture.

Top with the crumbs. Put a dab of margarine on each. Bake at 350°F (180°C) Gas Mark 4 for about 30 minutes.

The following dish requires preparation in advance, but at mealtime it needs only deep-frying.

• *Tempeh croquettes with mushroom sauce* •

1 lb tempeh
2 oz ($\frac{1}{4}$ cup) vegetable margarine
2 oz ($\frac{1}{2}$ cup) wholemeal flour
$\frac{1}{2}$ pint ($1\frac{1}{3}$ cups) soya milk
2 spring onions (scallions)
2 tablespoons soya flour
1 tablespoon soya sauce
3 teaspoons lemon juice
Sea salt and freshly ground black pepper
2 tablespoons gram (chickpea) flour
4 tablespoons water
4 oz (2 cups) fresh breadcrumbs
Oil for deep-frying
For the sauce:
4 oz mushrooms
2 tablespoons vegetable oil
3 tablespoons wholemeal flour
8 fl oz (1 cup) water
2-3 teaspoons Miso-Cup (see p. 106)

Steam the tempeh for about 15 minutes. Set aside.

Heat the margarine, stir in the flour, then gradually stir in the soya milk, stirring constantly to avoid lumps. When it has thickened remove from heat and mash the tempeh into this. Return to heat and stir well for a further minute. Remove from heat.

Chop the spring onions (scallions) finely and add to the mixture. Stir in the soya flour, soya sauce, lemon juice and seasoning. Spread out on a plate to cool, then shape into croquettes.

Beat the gram flour into the water with a fork. Dip the croquettes into the breadcrumbs, then into the gram flour mixture, and then once again into the breadcrumbs. Leave the croquettes for two hours or longer, to allow the croquettes to dry out so that the breadcrumbs will adhere to them when deep-fried.

When ready to serve, just heat up the oil and deep-fry the croquettes until nicely browned. Serve with mushroom sauce and cooked vegetables or salad.

To make the sauce, chop the mushrooms finely. Sauté in the oil for a few minutes. Stir in the flour, then gradually add the water, stirring constantly to avoid lumps. When boiling and thickened, lower heat and stir in Miso-Cup. Serve immediately.

American-style tempeh hash

1 pint (2½ cups) water
4 teaspoons yeast extract
1 lb tempeh
1 onion
1 green pepper
2 sticks celery
3 tablespoons vegetable oil
3 tablespoons wholemeal flour
2 tablespoons tomato ketchup
Freshly ground black pepper
Toast as required

Heat ½ pint (1¼ cups) water and dissolve 2 teaspoons yeast extract in it. Place the tempeh in the saucepan, lower heat, and simmer for 5-7 minutes before turning over and simmering for a further 5-7 minutes on the other side. The liquid should have mostly been absorbed by now, but if there is any left drain it. Chop the tempeh finely and set aside.

Chop the onion, green pepper and celery finely. Bring the remaining ½ pint (1¼ cups) water to the boil, and add the vegetables. Lower heat and simmer for a few minutes until tender. Drain the vegetables, retaining the stock.

Heat the oil in a large saucepan and stir in the flour. Slowly stir in the vegetable water and when it has thickened add the remaining 2 teaspoons yeast extract and the ketchup. Add the vegetables and tempeh and stir well. Season to taste with black pepper (salt should not be necessary), and serve on hot toast.

Tempeh hash with potatoes

1 lb potatoes
1 lb tempeh
1 pint (2½ cups) water
4 teaspoons yeast extract
1 onion
1 green pepper
4 tablespoons vegetable oil
2 tablespoons wholemeal flour
2 tablespoons tomato purée (paste)
Freshly ground black pepper

Cook the potatoes. Cook the tempeh in ½ pint (1⅔ cups) water and 2 teaspoons yeast extract as described in the previous recipe. (If desired, these processes can be carried out in advance, and the tempeh and potato then kept refrigerated until ready to prepare the dish.)

Chop the onion and green pepper finely. Fry in the oil for 3-4 minutes until beginning to brown.

Dice the tempeh and potato and add them to the saucepan. Cook for a minute or two longer, stirring constantly. Add the flour and stir well, then slowly pour in the remaining water, stirring constantly. Stir in the remaining yeast extract, the tomato purée and pepper. Heat thoroughly and serve.

• *Savoury tempeh loaf** •

1 lb tempeh
1 onion
1 green pepper
3 sticks celery
4 oz (½ cup) tomato
  purée (paste)

5 tablespoons water
2 oz (1 cup) fresh
  wholemeal
  breadcrumbs
Few drops Tabasco
  sauce (optional)

Steam the tempeh for about 15 minutes.

Chop the onion, green pepper, and celery very finely.

Mash the steamed tempeh in a large bowl, and add the finely chopped vegetables, the tomato purée (paste), water and breadcrumbs. Mix well. Sprinkle in the Tabasco sauce if using. (If desired add a little sea salt, but taste the mixture first as tomato purée is quite salty.)

Bake the loaf in an oiled tin or baking dish at 350°F (180°C) Gas Mark 4 for 45 minutes to an hour. Serve with seasonal vegetables.

* This recipe appeared in *The Vegetarian* Jan/Feb 1987.

As mentioned in the introduction to this section, tempeh originates in Indonesia. When I began writing this book I expected to have a large chunk of this section devoted to Indonesian dishes. However, when I came to research them I discovered that they virtually all contain ingredients which are not, at this stage, readily available in the UK. I therefore offer only one recipe, and even that has been much adapted to include only readily-available items.

• *Indonesian-style tempeh* •

12 oz tempeh
8 oz potatoes
2 teaspoons coriander seeds
1 onion
1 clove garlic
2 tablespoons vegetable oil
1 teaspoon turmeric
1 teaspoon sea salt
1 teaspoon raw sugar
1 teaspoon lemon juice
1 teaspoon finely grated fresh ginger
1 pint (2½ cups) water
4 oz cabbage
1 oz creamed coconut
Brown rice as required.

Cube the tempeh. Cut the potatoes into small pieces. Set aside.

Grind the coriander in a pestle and mortar. Grate the onion. Crush the garlic. Heat the vegetable oil in a large saucepan. Add the coriander, turmeric, onion, garlic, salt, sugar, lemon juice and ginger. Stir for a minute. Add the tempeh and potatoes, and stir for another minute or two. Add the water, bring to the boil, lower heat, cover and simmer for about 10 minutes.

Shred the cabbage. Grate or finely chop the creamed coconut. Add these ingredients to the saucepan. Cover and cook for a further 5-10 minutes until the potatoes are thoroughly cooked.

Serve over brown rice. (Lovers of spicy food could serve Sambal Oelek with this, an Indonesian chilli relish found at many delicatessens.)

Tempeh is unknown in the Middle East, but it works well in place of a non-vegetarian ingredient in traditional dishes.

See back of book

· Middle Eastern-style tempeh and · aubergine stew

> 2 small or 1 large (about 1 lb) aubergines (eggplants)
> 1 onion
> 4 tablespoons vegetable oil
> 2 tablespoons soya sauce
> $\frac{3}{4}$ pint (2 cups) + 4 tablespoons water
> 1 lb tempeh
> 3 tomatoes
>
> 2 tablespoons tomato purée (paste)
> 2 teaspoons ground cumin
> 2 teaspoons ground allspice
> Juice of 1 small (or $\frac{1}{2}$ large) lemon
> Sea salt and freshly ground black pepper

Slice the aubergines (eggplants), salt them and place them on a colander with a kitchen towel and weight on top of them for at least half an hour.

Chop the onion and sauté it in 2 tablespoons oil until tender.

Combine the soya sauce with the 4 tablespoons water in a shallow bowl. Dip the tempeh briefly in this mixture on both sides, drain on kitchen towels, then dice. Add the diced tempeh to the onion, and stir over a moderately high flame until lightly browned.

Peel and chop the tomatoes and add to the saucepan, along with the tomatoe purée (paste), cumin, allspice, lemon juice and seasonings. Stir well, then pour in the $\frac{3}{4}$ pint (2 cups) water and bring to the boil. Cover, lower heat and leave to simmer.

Rinse the aubergines (eggplants) well and pat dry. Fry the slices in the other 2 tablespoons oil in a frying pan until lightly browned. Add them to the saucepan and stir well.

Leave the stew to simmer, covered, for about half an hour. Serve with brown rice or bread.

· *Middle Eastern-style tempeh* ·
and okra stew

2 onions
2 cloves garlic
1 oz ($\frac{1}{8}$ cup) vegetable margarine
1 lb tempeh
1 lb okra
8 oz tomatoes
2 teaspoons ground coriander
2 tablespoons tomato purée (paste)
$\frac{3}{4}$ pint (2 cups) water
Juice of 1 lemon
Sea salt and freshly ground black pepper

Chop the onions. Chop the garlic finely. Sauté the onion and garlic in the margarine until beginning to turn brown.

Cube the tempeh. Add to the saucepan and fry for a few minutes longer.

Clean, then top and tail the okra (larger ones may be halved). Add the prepared okra to the saucepan and stir well.

Peel and chop the tomatoes. Add to the saucepan along with the coriander. Stir well. Stir in the tomato purée (paste) and water. Bring to the boil, lower heat then simmer for about half an hour. Just before serving, add lemon juice and seasoning to taste.

Serve with brown rice or bread.

• Middle Eastern-style tempeh balls •

2 tablespoons water
2 tablespoons soya sauce
1 lb tempeh
1½ teaspoons cinnamon
Freshly ground black pepper to taste
2 onions
2 tablespoons vegetable oil
2 oz pine nuts
1 5-oz tin tomato purée (paste)
Juice of 1 small lemon
Brown rice as required
2 tablespoons minced parsley

Pour the water and soya sauce into a saucepan, bring to the boil, then lower the tempeh into it. Cook for 5-7 minutes on one side, then turn it over and cook for a further 5-7 minutes on the other. Drain and cool.

Put the tempeh through a grinder (or food processor), then transfer the paste to a mixing bowl. Add cinnamon and a little pepper, and knead well, then shape into walnut-sized balls.

Slice the onions thinly and sauté briefly in the oil. Add the tempeh balls and stir gently. Add the pine nuts and cook for a further minute or two.

Mix the tomato purée (paste) with some water and add it to the saucepan. Add enough additional water to cover the balls. Add the lemon juice and a little more pepper as well (salt should not be necessary). Bring to the boil, then cover and simmer for about 15 minutes, stirring occasionally (very gently).

Serve over brown rice, with the parsley spinkled on top.

Moroccan-style tempeh brochettes

1 lb tempeh
1 onion
3 tablespoons minced parsley
2 teaspoons ground cumin
1 teaspoon freshly ground black pepper
1 teaspoon dried marjoram
2 teaspoons ground coriander
2 teaspoons soya sauce
$\frac{1}{2}$ teaspoon Harissa*

Grind the tempeh, then transfer the paste to a mixing bowl.

Grate the onion and add it to the paste along with all the other ingredients. Knead the mixture very well. Shape small lumps of the mixture round skewers (preferably the flat-edged 'sword' type), and place under a very hot grill (broiler). Cook until one side is well browned, then turn over and cook until the other side is also well browned. (NB It is not that easy to persuade these tempeh lumps to remain on the skewers; if preferred they can be placed directly on a grill pan and turned once manually.)

Serve the brochettes in pitta bread or over brown rice, with a salad. If very spicy food is liked, then thin down some Harissa with water and use that to pour over the brochettes.

* Available at Middle Eastern and Asian shops and some delicatessens

• Part Four •

MISO

MISO

Miso is another fermented soya food, but it is different from the others featured in this book, as it is used primarily as a flavouring ingredient. It is a thick dark paste. Miso is high in protein, and the fermentation process renders it as good for the digestion as yogurt. Ideally, miso should be added to dishes at the last possible moment – or eaten uncooked – because boiling destroys the valuable digestion-aiding enzymes. Unlike tempeh, miso will keep for a long time. It is such a highly concentrated food that only a small amount is needed for any dish. After opening, miso can be transferred to a jar, or it can be kept in its original plastic bag, if that is folded over to keep air out (a rubber band can be useful for this purpose). It can then be kept in the larder or fridge for many months.

In Japan – the home of miso – there are an enormous number of different varieties. Some British wholefood and macrobiotic shops are importing some of them, so the connoisseur is finding a much wider choice nowadays. Amongst these is a sweet white miso, which is very different from the types of miso previously known in this country; as it is still relatively hard to find in Britain, I have not used it in any of the recipes in this book.

All misos are made from soya beans, either on their

own or with another primary ingredient. The three basic types found in British health food and wholefood shops are pure soya bean (*hatcho*) miso, barley miso, and rice miso. *Hatcho* miso is darker and saltier than the other two and also much more solid (and therefore more difficult to blend into dishes). Barley miso is redder, softer and mellower in flavour; rice miso is redder and mellower still. Any of the three can be used interchangeably in the recipes that follow, though quantities may need to be adjusted for the different varieties – in recipes which call for a larger amount the chances are that I used barley or rice miso, while in those calling for a smaller amount I probably used *hatcho*. In any case, individual tastes differ so greatly in respect of a salty seasoning like miso that it is best to use the suggested amounts as a rough guide only.

Miso can also be found in a powdered form, sold in sachets under the brand name Miso-Cup (plain or with seaweed). Mixed with hot water it makes a quick savoury nutritious soup-in-a-cup.

The most popular dish containing miso is, without question, soup. Miso soup is a staple of the Japanese diet as well as of the macrobiotic diet of many in the West. Naturally the miso is added only after the rest of the ingredients have cooked. The first recipe is a version of the classic Japanese/macrobiotic soup. Those which follow show how miso can be used in Western-style soups as well.

• *Miso soup with cabbage and carrot* •

1 onion
2 tablespoons vegetable oil
2 carrots
1 small cabbage (1 lb or slightly less)
1½ pints (3¾ cups) water
2 tablespoons miso

Chop the onion and sauté in the vegetable oil for 2-3 minutes.

Slice the carrots into thin short matchsticks. Chop the cabbage. Add to the saucepan, stirring well, and cook for a further 3-4 minutes.

Add the water and bring to the boil. Lower heat and leave to simmer for about 20 minutes.

Remove a little of the soup stock and mix it in a cup with the miso, creaming it well. Return to the saucepan, stir well and serve.

Cream of mushroom miso soup

1 lb mushrooms
1 onion
2 sticks celery
2 oz ($\frac{1}{8}$ cup) vegetable margarine
$\frac{3}{4}$ pint (2 cups) water or vegetable stock
2 tablespoons miso
2 tablespoons wholemeal flour
$\frac{3}{4}$ pint (2 cups) soya milk
Freshly ground black pepper to taste
3 tablespoons minced parsley

Chop the mushrooms, onion and celery. Melt half the margarine in a saucepan and add the vegetables. Sauté for about 3 minutes. Add the water or stock, bring to the boil, then lower heat, cover the saucepan, and simmer for about 10 minutes.

Pour the mixture into a liquidizer along with the miso, and leave to cool slightly. Blend thoroughly.

Meanwhile, melt the remainder of the margarine and stir in the flour. Gradually stir in the soya milk, very slowly to avoid lumps, and bring to the boil. Boil for a minute or two, then lower heat to the barest minimum and pour in the contents of the liquidizer. Season with pepper, and serve topped with the parsley.

• Vegetable soup with miso •

2 carrots
4-6 oz white turnip
4 sticks celery
2 onions
1½ pints (4 cups) water

1 oz (¼ cup) broken cashews
2 tablespoons miso
1 teaspoon garlic salt
2 tablespoons parsley
1 teaspoon dried basil

Chop the carrots, turnip, celery and onion. Put them in the water in a saucepan. Bring to the boil, then lower heat, cover and simmer for about 15 minutes.

Pour about half the liquid and vegetables (the precise quantity doesn't matter at all) into a liquidizer; leave to cool slightly. Add the cashews, miso, garlic salt, parsley and basil and blend well.

Pour the blended mixture into the unblended soup, stir well and reheat very gently. Serve immediately.

Sandwich spreads are a particularly good way of using miso because they require no cooking at all. Below are three suggestions.

• Soya 'cream cheese' spread •

8 oz soya 'cream cheese' (see p. 7) 4 teaspoons miso

Stir the miso into the 'cream cheese' and mix thoroughly.

• Lentil and parsley spread •

6 oz (1 cup) red lentils
¾ pint (2 cups) water
3 teaspoons miso
4 tablespoons minced parsley
A little freshly grated nutmeg

Wash the lentils, put them in a saucepan, and cover with the water. Bring to the boil, then lower heat, cover the pan, and simmer for about 15 minutes, by which time the water should have been absorbed and the lentils become a thick purée.

Remove from heat and immediately beat in the miso. Then add the parsley and nutmeg, and mix thoroughly.

Leave to cool before serving.

• Tahini spread •

4 tablespoons tahini
3 teaspoons miso
1 teaspoon finely grated orange rind

Combine all the ingredients and mix thoroughly.

Lentil pâté

4 oz (2 cups) wholemeal bread
4 oz (⅔ cup) red lentils
½ pint (1⅓ cups) water
1 onion
2 tablespoons vegetable oil
1 tablespoon tahini
1 teaspoon dried rosemary
½ teaspoon dried thyme
Pinch nutmeg
1 tablespoon minced parsley
1 tablespoon miso

Break the bread up into pieces, cover with water, and leave to soak for about an hour.

Cook the lentils in the ½ pint (1⅓ cups) water for about 15 minutes until tender.

Chop the onion. Sauté it in the oil for about 5 minutes, until tender and beginning to brown.

Add the onions to the lentils. Drain the bread and squeeze as much moisture out as possible; add to the lentils and onions. Stir in the tahini, rosemary, thyme and nutmeg, and cook over low heat for about 5 minutes.

Stir in the parsley and miso, beating well to amalgamate it into the mixture. Turn into an oiled baking dish, and bake for about half an hour at 350°F (180°C) Gas Mark 4. Serve warm or cold.

Miso makes wonderful gravy for nut roasts and other savouries. The easiest way is to use Miso-Cup (see p. 106) as that dissolves instantly.

• *Miso gravy 1* •

2 tablespoons vegetable oil
3 tablespoons wholemeal flour

1 pint ($2\frac{1}{2}$ cups) water
1 envelope Miso-Cup

Heat the oil in a saucepan. Gradually stir in the flour and cook for about 30 seconds. Carefully stir in the water, as slowly as possible to avoid lumps. Bring to the boil. Stir in Miso-Cup and serve.

The recipe can be varied by sautéing finely chopped mushrooms or onions in the oil before stirring in the flour. It can be made thicker if desired by using less water.

The following is the simplest way I know of making gravy from miso itself. Once again it can be made thicker or thinner if desired, by varying the proportions of water and thickener.

• Miso gravy 2 •

¾ pint (2 cups) lukewarm water
4 teaspoons miso

6 teaspoons cornflour (cornstarch)

Put the lukewarm water, miso and cornflour (cornstarch) in the liquidizer and blend thoroughly.

Pour the mixture into a saucepan, and heat at very low temperature, stirring constantly, until thickened. Let simmer for a minute or so, then serve immediately.

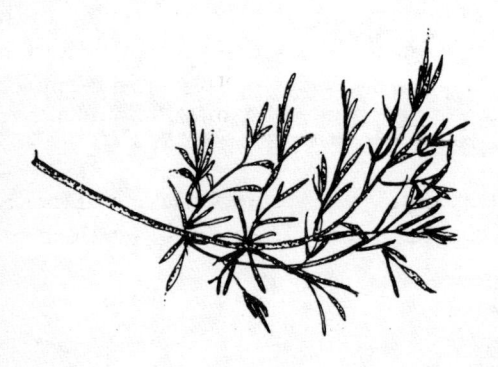

Miso adds a superb flavour to stews.

• *Cashew nut ragoût* •

6-8 oz (1-1⅓ cups) whole cashews
2 onions
3 tablespoons vegetable oil
4 tomatoes
8 oz mushrooms
2 oz (½ cup) wholemeal flour
½ pint (1⅓ cups) water or vegetable stock
¼ teaspoon thyme
3 teaspoons miso

Toast the cashews under the grill (broiler), turning them until they are nicely browned. Set aside.

Slice the onions thinly and sauté in the oil for 2-3 minutes. Slice the tomatoes and mushrooms and add to the saucepan. Sauté until the vegetables are tender.

Stir the flour into the saucepan. Slowly add the water or stock, stirring constantly, and bring to the boil. Stir in the thyme, and then stir in the miso, a little at a time to avoid lumps.

Finally, stir in the whole cashews. Serve with boiled, baked or mashed potatoes and a green vegetable.

Bean and potato stew

1½ lb potatoes
2 onions
2 tablespoons vegetable oil
½ pint (1⅓ cups) vegetable stock or water
1 tablespoon minced parsley
1 teaspoon dried sage
2 15-oz tins (or 10 oz/2½ cups cooked, drained) butter (Lima) beans
1 tablespoon miso

Cook the potatoes in lightly salted boiling water until tender. Drain and chop.

Slice the onions thinly. Sauté in the oil for a few minutes until lightly browned.

Stir in the stock or water, the parsley and the sage. Then stir in the drained beans. Bring to the boil and simmer for 2-3 minutes.

Stir in the potatoes and simmer for a further 2-3 minutes.

Remove a little of the stock from the saucepan and cream it with the miso in a cup before stirring it into the saucepan.

Serve immediately, either over brown rice or in a bowl accompanied by wholemeal bread.

• Vegetable stew •

2 carrots
8 oz turnips or swedes
3 tablespoons vegetable oil
8 oz cabbage
2 leeks
2 onions
2 potatoes
2 tomatoes
2 bay leaves
½ pint (1⅓ cups) vegetable stock or water
1-2 tablespoons miso

Chop the carrots and turnips coarsely. Heat the oil in a large saucepan and sauté them for 3-4 minutes.

Chop the cabbage coarsely. Slice the leeks and onions. Add them to the saucepan and cook for another 3-4 minutes.

Chop the potatoes into fairly small chunks. Add them to the saucepan with the quartered tomatoes. Mix well and add the bay leaves and stock or water. Bring to the boil, lower heat, cover pan and simmer for about 25 minutes, until the potatoes are tender (the one vegetable that does not taste better a little 'al dente' is potato).

Take out the bay leaves.

Remove a little of the liquid from the saucepan into a cup and add the miso to it; cream it well then return it to the saucepan. Mix well and serve with wholemeal bread.

Deep-fried rice balls with sweet and sour vegetables

For the balls:
10 oz (1⅔ cup) short-grain brown rice
4-5 spring onions (scallions)
2 cloves garlic
3 tablespoons miso
3 tablespoons tahini
3 teaspoons minced fresh ginger
Cornflour (cornstarch) as required
Oil for deep-frying

For the sauce:
1 large onion
2 tablespoons vegetable oil
1 green pepper
1 carrot
1 8-oz tin pineapple chunks in juice
3-4 teaspoons raw sugar
1 tablespoon cider vinegar
2 tablespoons soya sauce
6 tablespoons water
1 tablespoon cornflour (cornstarch)

To make the balls, cook the rice until tender and cool slightly. Mince the spring onions (scallions) and crush the garlic, then add them, along with the miso, tahini and ginger, to the rice. Mix very thoroughly

Cover the bottom of a plate with cornflour (cornstarch). Form the rice mixture into balls about the size of a walnut or a little larger, and roll in the cornflour (cornstarch). Actually, it is easier, as the mixture is rather sloppy and sticky, to transfer a spoonful at a time of mixture to the plate, then roll it into a ball with the help of the cornflour (cornstarch) adhering to it. Deep-fry the balls until brown and crisp.

To make the sauce, chop the onion finely and sauté in the oil for about 2 minutes. Chop the green pepper finely and grate the carrot coarsely. Add them to the saucepan and continue cooking for a further 2-3 minutes. Then add the pineapple chunks along with the pineapple juice from the tin, the sugar, vinegar, soya sauce, and 3 tablespoons of the water. Bring to the boil, then lower heat, cover and simmer for a few minutes. Dissolve the cornflour (cornstarch) in the remaining 3 tablespoons water and stir it into the vegetables until thickened.

The topping below could be used for a conventional pizza as well. But this recipe certainly is a time-saver.

• Quick pizza •

7 oz (1¾ cup) wholemeal flour
5 tablespoons vegetable oil
Pinch sea salt
2 teaspoons baking powder
1 onion
2 tablespoons tomato purée (paste)
5 tablespoons water
2 teaspoons dried oregano
Half a dozen black olives
1 tablespoon tahini
1 tablespoon miso

Mix the flour with 1 tablespoon oil, salt and baking powder; add sufficient water to make a soft dough. Roll out into two 7-inch circles for the bases.

Chop the onion finely. Fry in 2 tablespoons oil until tender. Mix the tomato purée (paste), 2 tablespoons water, oregano and the onion in a small bowl.

Chop the olives finely.

Mix the tahini, miso and remaining 3 tablespoons water in a small bowl.

Heat 1 tablespoon oil in a large frying pan. Fry one of the bases for 4-5 minutes, then turn over. Spread with half the tomato mixture, sprinkle with half the olives, and top with half the tahini mixture. Cook for a further 4-5 minutes, then place under a medium grill (broiler) until the tahini is browned. Repeat with the second base. Serve with a green salad.

• *Part Five* •

COMBI-DISHES

· 1 ·
Tofu and miso

The salty tang of miso is the perfect complement to bland tofu.

· *Tofu and miso dip/spread* ·

1 lb (2 cups) tofu	1 tablespoon vegetable oil
2 spring onions (scallions)	1 tablespoon soya milk
1 tablespoon minced parsley	1 teaspoon soya sauce
3 teaspoons lemon juice	1 tablespoon miso
	Freshly ground black pepper to taste

Put 12 oz (1½ cups) tofu into a bowl and mash it with a fork. Chop the spring onions (scallions) finely and add, along with the parsley, to the bowl.

Put the remaining 4 oz (½ cup) tofu into a liquidizer, along with the lemon juice, oil, soya milk and soya sauce, and blend thoroughly. Add the miso and blend again.

Add the liquidizer mixture to the bowl and mix well. Add pepper. Serve chilled as a party dip or as a sandwich spread.

Tofu and miso casserole

1 lb (2 cups) tofu
Oil for deep-frying
2 small onions or 1 large
2 cloves garlic
1½ oz vegetable margarine
1 oz (¼ cup) wholemeal flour
½ pint (1⅓ cups) soya milk
2 tablespoons miso
Freshly ground black pepper to taste
2 oz (1 cup) fresh wholemeal breadcrumbs

Cube the tofu and deep-fry until golden. (This may be done in advance, and the cubes kept in the fridge until cooking time.)

Slice the onions thinly. Crush the garlic. Sauté in 1 oz (⅛ cup) of the margarine for 4-5 minutes, until softened and lightly browned.

Stir the flour into the onions. Gradually add the soya milk, stirring constantly to avoid lumps. Bring to the boil and when thickened remove from the heat. Immediately stir in the miso, and continue stirring well until smooth. Add pepper to taste, then stir in the tofu cubes.

Turn the mixture into an oiled baking dish, sprinkle with the breadcrumbs, dot with the remaining margarine, and bake in a 350°F (180°C) Gas Mark 4 oven for about 20 minutes.

Spaghetti with tofu and miso sauce

1 lb (2 cups) tofu
2 tablespoons vegetable oil + more for deep-frying
2 onions
2 cloves garlic
4 oz mushrooms
2 sticks celery
12 oz tomatoes
2 carrots
4 fluid oz ($\frac{1}{2}$ cup) tomato ketchup
$\frac{1}{4}$ pint ($\frac{2}{3}$ cup) water
2 bay leaves
Freshly ground black pepper
12 oz wholemeal spaghetti
$\frac{1}{2}$ oz vegetable margarine
3 teaspoons miso
2 tablespoons hot water

Cut the tofu into small cubes and deep-fry until golden. Set aside.

Chop the onions coarsely and the garlic finely. Sauté in the vegetable oil for 2-3 minutes.

Chop the mushrooms, celery and tomatoes. Grate the carrots. Add to the onion, stir, and cook for a further 2-3 minutes. Add the ketchup, water, bay leaves, pepper and tofu. Bring to the boil, then lower heat and simmer for about 15 minutes.

Meanwhile, cook the spaghetti until tender, drain and toss with the margarine.

Cream the miso in a cup with the hot water and add to the tofu sauce. Simmer for another minute, then remove from heat and serve over the spaghetti.

· Tangy noodle casserole* ·

10 oz wholemeal noodles
1 lb (2 cups) tofu
1½ tablespoons lemon juice
1 tablespoon vegetable oil
2 tablespoons miso
3 spring onions (scallions)
1 tablespoon vegetable margarine

Cook the noodles until tender in lightly salted water and drain.

Put half the tofu in a liquidizer along with the lemon juice, oil and miso, and blend thoroughly.

Put the other half of the tofu into a tea towel (dish towel) and squeeze as much of the moisture out as possible.

Chop the spring onions (scallions) finely.

In a large bowl combine the noodles, tofu/miso mixture, squeezed tofu and chopped spring onions (scallions). Mix well, then turn into an oiled casserole.

Dot the top of the casserole with small pieces of margarine, cover and bake at 350°F (180°C) Gas Mark 4 for 20 minutes, then uncover and bake for a further 10 minutes. Serve immediately, accompanied by seasonal vegetables.

* This recipe appeared in *Green Cuisine* Sept/Oct 1986.

Macaroni, mushroom and tofu casserole

8 oz (1 cup) tofu
Oil for deep-frying
8 oz wholemeal macaroni (any shape)
8 oz mushrooms
4 tablespoons vegetable margarine
2 teaspoons lemon juice
3 tablespoons wholemeal flour
$\frac{1}{2}$ pint ($1\frac{1}{3}$ cups) soya milk
2 teaspoons miso
Freshly ground black pepper to taste
Good-Tasting Yeast (see p. 37) as required (optional)

Cube the tofu and deep-fry until golden. Set aside.

Cook the macaroni until tender and set aside.

Slice the mushrooms and sauté them in 1 tablespoon margarine until just tender. Sprinkle the lemon juice over them and set aside.

Melt the remainder of the margarine in a saucepan, and stir in the flour. Slowly add the soya milk, stirring constantly to avoid lumps. Remove from heat, and stir in miso and pepper.

Add the cooked macaroni, fried tofu cubes, and sautéed mushrooms to the sauce, and mix well. Turn into an oiled casserole, sprinkle with Good-Tasting Yeast if used, and place in the oven at 350°F (180°C) Gas Mark 4 for about 15 minutes. Serve with steamed seasonal vegetables or salad.

Millet and vegetable savoury

8 oz (1 cup) millet
1½ pints (3¾ cups) water
Sea salt to taste
4 small or 2 large leeks
2 carrots
4 sticks celery
2 oz (½ cup) vegetable margarine
12 oz (1½ cups) tofu
2 tablespoons tahini
1½ tablespoons miso
Juice of 1 small lemon
2 teaspoons soya sauce
4 tablespoons soya yogurt
6 tablespoons water

Wash the millet, cover with the water (lightly salted to taste), bring to the boil, lower heat, cover and simmer until all the water is absorbed (about 30 minutes).

Meanwhile, chop the leeks and grate the carrots coarsely. Melt the margarine in a frying pan and sauté the vegetables for about 10 minutes, stirring frequently.

Put the tofu, tahini, miso, lemon juice, soya sauce, soya yogurt and water in a liquidizer and blend thoroughly.

Mix the vegetables into the millet. Pour about three-quarters of the tofu mixture in and mix thoroughly. Pour this mixture into a greased casserole, and pour the remainder of the tofu mixture over the top.

Bake at 375°F (190°C) Gas Mark 5 for 20-30 minutes, until the top is nicely browned.

Lentil loaf with tofu topping

8 oz (1⅓ cups) red lentils
8 fl oz (1 cup) water
1 onion
4 teaspoons miso
1 tablespoon tahini
2 teaspoons lemon juice
6 oz (¾ cup) tofu
2 tablespoons soya milk
1 tablespoon vegetable oil

Wash the lentils well, cover them with the water, bring to the boil, lower heat and simmer for about 15 minutes until tender and the water is absorbed.

Chop the onion very finely.

When the lentils are cooked, beat the miso in. Then add the tahini, lemon juice, and onion. Turn into a greased loaf tin or baking dish.
Put the tofu, soya milk and oil in a liquidizer and blend thoroughly.

Spread the tofu mixture on top of the lentil mixture as evenly as possible. Bake in a 375°F (190°C) Gas Mark 5 oven for about 45 minutes, until lightly browned and firm. Serve with potatoes, grilled tomatoes or a tomato sauce, and a green vegetable.

· Warming winter stew ·

1 lb (2 cups) medium or firm tofu
2 tablespoons vegetable oil + additional for deep-frying
2 onions
8 oz carrots
8 oz Savoy cabbage
1 tablespoon sesame oil*
1 pint ($2\frac{1}{2}$ cups) vegetable stock or water
2-3 tablespoons miso
1 teaspoon arrowroot
1 tablespoon water

Cube the tofu and deep-fry until golden brown. Drain and set aside.

Slice the onions thinly. Chop the carrots and cabbage. Sauté the vegetables in the oils for a minute or two. Add the deep-fried tofu cubes and the stock or water. Bring to the boil, cover and reduce heat. Leave to simmer for about 10 minutes.

Remove a little of the hot liquid and use it to cream the miso before stirring it into the saucepan. Dissolve the arrowroot in the tablespoon water and stir into the saucepan until thickened.

Serve immediately, either with brown rice or accompanied by wholemeal bread.

* Available at Chinese shops.

• Jambalaya •

10 oz (1⅔ cups) brown rice
8 oz (1 cup) medium or firm tofu
2 onions
3 tablespoons vegetable oil
4 sticks celery
1 green pepper
4 oz mushrooms
2 tomatoes
2 tablespoons miso
2 teaspoons paprika
A few drops Tabasco sauce
1 oz parsley

Cook the rice until tender.

Cube the tofu and deep-fry the cubes until golden brown.

Chop the onions and sauté in the oil for 2-3 minutes. Chop the celery, green pepper and mushrooms, and add to the onion. Cook for a further minute or two. Chop the tomatoes and add to the pan; cook for 2-3 minutes longer. Then stir in the deep-fried tofu cubes.

Remove the saucepan from the heat, and stir in the cooked rice, miso, paprika, and Tabasco sauce. Mix well, and turn into an oiled casserole. Bake at 300°F 150°C (Gas Mark 2) for about 45 minutes.

Chop the parsley finely, and sprinkle over the dish just before serving.

· 2 ·
Tempeh and tofu

The creaminess of tofu goes beautifully with the flavour and 'bite' of tempeh — and of course tempeh adds fibre to such dishes.

· *Tempeh spread* ·

8 oz tempeh
1 largish onion
2 cloves garlic
2 tablespoons vegetable oil
4 tablespoons Smokey Snaps*

1 teaspoon oregano
5 tablespoons finely chopped fresh parsley
5-6 tablespoons tofu mayonnaise

Steam the tempeh. Mash it in a mixing bowl.

Chop the onion finely. Crush the garlic. Sauté the onion and garlic in the oil in a frying pan for 3-5 minutes until lightly browned.

Add the fried onion and garlic to the tempeh, along with the Smokey Snaps, oregano, parsley, and tofu mayonnaise. Mix thoroughly. Chill before serving.

* Available at most health food stores.

· Tempeh stroganoff ·

2 cloves garlic
4 tablespoons vegetable oil
3 tablespoons soya sauce
¼ pint (⅔ cups) apple juice
½ teaspoon ground ginger
½ teaspoon paprika
Freshly ground black pepper to taste

1 lb tempeh
12 oz mushrooms
2 tablespoons vegetable margarine
½ teaspoon dried basil
A little freshly grated nutmeg
8 oz (1 cup) tofu
Juice of 1 small lemon

Crush the garlic. Combine in a large saucepan 2 tablespoons oil, the soya sauce, apple juice, ginger, paprika, pepper and the garlic. Cube the tempeh. Add to the mixture in the saucepan and cook over a low heat for about 5 minutes, stirring occasionally.

Slice the mushrooms. Melt the margarine in a frying pan and add the mushrooms. Sprinkle in the basil, and grate in a little nutmeg. Stir over a medium-low heat for about 5 minutes until tender. Add the mushrooms to the tempeh and stir well.

Put the tofu, remaining 2 tablespoons oil, and lemon juice in a liquidizer and blend thoroughly. Add the mixture to the tempeh and mushroom mixture, and heat over a low heat until it is warmed through.

Serve over cooked wholemeal noodles.

Curried stir-fried noodles with tempeh and tofu

8 oz Chinese noodles
12 oz tempeh
2 tablespoons vegetable oil (+ additional for deep-frying)
8 oz (1 cup) medium or firm tofu
1 teaspoon turmeric
½ teaspoon garlic salt
1 onion
4 oz carrots
4 oz cabbage
4 oz mushrooms
1 or 2 spring onions (scallions)
2 teaspoons curry powder
1 tablespoon soya sauce

Cook the noodles in boiling water until tender. Drain, pour cold water over them and set aside.

Dice the tempeh and deep-fry. Set aside.

Mash the tofu in a bowl with the turmeric and garlic salt. Set aside.

Chop the onion and stir-fry in the 2 tablespoons oil for 2-3 minutes.

Grate the carrots coarsely. Shred the cabbage. Chop the mushrooms and spring onions (scallions). Add to the onions and stir-fry for a further 2-3 minutes.

Stir in the curry powder and then the tofu mixture. Continue stir-frying for 1-2 minutes longer. Then stir in the noodles and soya sauce, mix well, and continue stir-frying until the noodles are well heated. Finally, stir in the tempeh cubes, and cook for a minute or two longer until the cubes are heated. Serve immediately.

Courgette and tomato stew with dumplings

2 onions
3 tablespoons vegetable oil
3 cloves garlic
2 fresh chillies
2 tablespoons cumin seed
2 teaspoons ground cinnamon
6 oz tempeh
2 15-oz tins tomatoes
4 fl oz ($\frac{1}{2}$ cup) water
1 lb courgettes (zucchini)
8 oz (1 cup) medium or firm tofu
Sea salt and freshly ground black pepper

To make the dumplings:
6 oz (1 cup) maize meal (cornmeal)
2 oz ($\frac{1}{2}$ cup) wholemeal flour
1 oz ($\frac{1}{4}$ cup) soya flour
2 teaspoons baking powder
A little sea salt
$\frac{2}{3}$ pint ($1\frac{1}{2}$ cups) soya milk
1 tablespoon vegetable oil

Chop the onions and sauté in the oil in a large saucepan for 2-3 minutes. Mince the garlic and chillies; grind the cumin seeds. Add these ingredients to the saucepan, along with the cinnamon. Sauté for a minute or two longer.

Cube the tempeh. Add to the saucepan along with the tinned tomatoes and water. When boiling, cover the pan and lower the heat. Leave to simmer for 10-15 minutes.

Slice the courgettes (zucchini). Cube the tofu. Add these ingredients to the saucepan, and season to taste. Leave to simmer for a further 5 minutes.

To make the dumplings combine the maize meal (cornmeal), wholemeal flour, soya flour, baking powder and salt in a bowl. Mix the soya milk and oil together and stir into the dry mixture.

Drop the batter by tablespoons into the saucepan, trying to make certain they are all immersed in the liquid. Cover the pan again and simmer for 15 minutes before serving.

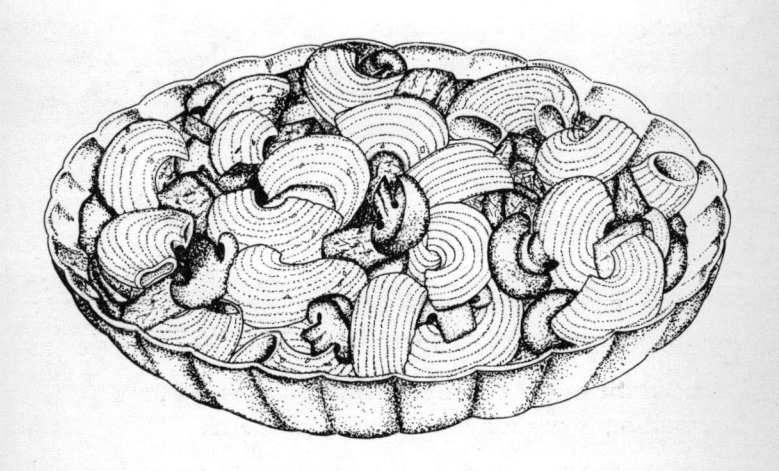

Stir-fried rice with tempeh and tofu*

12 oz (2 cups) brown rice
12 oz tempeh
8 oz (1 cup) tofu
2 teaspoons turmeric
4 spring onions (scallions)
2 cloves garlic
2 tablespoons vegetable oil
2 tablespoons soya sauce

Cook the rice until tender. (This may be done in advance and the rice kept in the refrigerator until ready to use.)

Cube and deep-fry the tempeh. (This may also be done in advance and the tempeh kept in the fridge until ready to use, but it will not have the same crisp texture as it would if fried immediately before preparing the dish.)

Mash the tofu with the turmeric. Mince the spring onions (scallions).

Mince the garlic finely. Heat the oil in a wok or large frying pan and add the garlic. Stir-fry for 30 seconds to a minute until lightly browned.

Add all the rest of the ingredients, and stir-fry until everything is sizzling hot. Serve immediately.

---

* This recipe appeared in *The Vegetarian* Jan/Feb 1987.

Savoury tempeh and tofu loaf

1 lb tempeh
8 tablespoons soya sauce
8 oz (2 cups) tofu
2 tablespoons vegetable oil
2 oz (1 cup) fresh wholemeal breadcrumbs
2 tablespoons minced parsley

Put the tempeh into a saucepan. Add enough water to cover and 6 tablespoons of the soya sauce. Bring to the boil, then cover, lower heat and simmer for about 15 minutes. Drain the tempeh and mash it.

Put the tofu into a liquidizer with the oil and remainder of the soya sauce, and blend thoroughly.

Pour the blended tofu over the mashed tempeh, stir in the breadcrumbs and parsley, and mix thoroughly. Transfer to an oiled baking dish or loaf tin. Bake at 375°F (190°C) Gas Mark 5 for 15-20 minutes. Serve with a tomato sauce and cooked seasonal vegetables.

Lasagne al forno

- 6 oz wholemeal lasagne
- 12 oz tempeh
- 2 onions
- 2 cloves garlic
- 2 tablespoons vegetable oil
- 4 oz mushrooms
- 2 15-oz tins tomatoes
- 4 tablespoons tomato purée (paste)
- 2 teaspoons oregano
- Freshly ground black pepper
- 1 lb (2 cups) tofu
- 3 tablespoons tahini
- 1 tablespoon soya sauce
- 2 tablespoons soya yogurt
- Juice of ½ lemon

Cook the lasagne in boiling salted water until tender. Drain.

Steam the tempeh (according to the instructions on pp. 86-7 or in a mixture of 4 parts water to 1 part soya sauce). Cool.

Chop the onions. Crush the garlic. Sauté in the oil in a saucepan for 3-4 minutes.

Chop the mushrooms finely. Add to the saucepan, along with the tomatoes, tomato purée (paste), and oregano. Bring to the boil, then lower heat and simmer, uncovered, for about 10 minutes. Crumble the tempeh into the saucepan, and continue simmering for about 10 minutes longer. Season to taste (additional salt should not be required).

Meanwhile, put the tofu, tahini, soya sauce, yogurt, and lemon juice in a liquidizer. Blend thoroughly.

Put alternate layers of lasagne, tempeh sauce, and blended tofu in a casserole, finishing with a layer of tofu. Bake at 350°F (180°C) Gas Mark 4 for 30 minutes. Serve with a green salad.

• Tofu and tempeh burgers •

8 oz tempeh
1 onion
1 clove garlic
1 tablespoon vegetable oil (+ additional for burgers)

8 oz (1 cup) tofu
3 tablespoons soya sauce
5 tablespoons wholemeal flour

Steam the tempeh. Cool.

Chop the onion and garlic finely and fry in the oil until lightly browned.

Mash the tempeh in a mixing bowl. Add and mash the tofu. Add the fried onion and garlic, the soya sauce, and the flour. Form into burgers (4 large or 8 small).

Fry in a little oil, turning over so the burgers are browned on both sides. Serve in a bun with the usual burger trimmings.

• Tempeh paprika •

2 onions
2 cloves garlic
2 tablespoons vegetable oil
1 lb tempeh
1 bay leaf
2 teaspoons dried thyme
2 tablespoons cider vinegar
$\frac{1}{2}$ pint ($1\frac{1}{3}$ cups) water
2 tablespoons paprika
1 tablespoon tomato purée (paste)
Sea salt and freshly ground black pepper
10 oz ($1\frac{1}{4}$ cups) tofu
3 teaspoons lemon juice
2 teaspoons vegetable oil
3 tablespoons soya milk
2 teaspoons soya sauce
3 teaspoons dried dill weed
Wholemeal noodles as required

Chop the onions and garlic very finely. Sauté in the 2 tablespoons oil until beginning to turn brown.

Cut the tempeh into cubes. Add to the saucepan and cook for another minute or two. Add the bay leaf, thyme, vinegar, water, paprika, tomato purée (paste) and salt and pepper. Stir gently but thoroughly. Bring to the boil, then lower heat and simmer for about half an hour; check after 20 minutes or so and if it is looking a bit dry then add 2-3 tablespoons more water.

Meanwhile, put the tofu, lemon juice, 2 teaspoons oil, soya milk and soya sauce in the liquidizer and blend until very smooth.

Add the tofu mixture and the dill weed to the saucepan and stir gently over very low heat until everything has warmed through. Serve immediately over cooked noodles.

INDEX

· A ·

American measurements, viii
American-style tempeh hash, 93

· B ·

Baked tofu slices, 34
Bean and potato stew, 116

· C ·

Cabbage and Chinese mushrooms with spiced pressed tofu, 67
Cabbage with spiced pressed tofu, 66
Carrot and spiced pressed tofu, 65
Cashew nut ragoût, 115
Central American style smokey pasta and bean dish, 73
Chilled cream of cucumber soup, 26
Courgette and tomato stew with dumplings, 135
Courgette, mushroom and rice savoury, 37
Cream of cauliflower and potato soup, 23
Cream of celery soup, 25
Cream of mushroom miso soup, 108
Creamy bean dip, 31
Curried stir-fried noodles with tempeh and tofu, 134

· D ·

Deep-fried rice balls with sweet and sour vegetables, 118
Desserts:
    Gooseberry fool, 41
    Hungarian-style layered pancakes, 45
    Maple walnut tofu ice cream, 48
    Pineapple cream, 40
    Raspberry tofu ice cream, 49
    Rhubarb fool, 43
    Strawberry 'cheese', 42
    Tofu strudel, 44
Devilled tofu and celery spread, 30

· G ·

Gooseberry fool, 41

· H ·

Hungarian-style layered pancakes, 45

· I ·

Indonesian-style tempeh, 96

· J ·

Jambalaya, 131

· L ·

Lasagne al forno, 141
Leek and smoked tofu au gratin, 78

Index

Lentil and parsley spread, 111
Lentil and smoked tofu soup, 69
Lentil loaf with tofu topping, 129
Lentil paté, 112
Lentil tofu with macaroni, 53

· M ·

Macaroni, mushroom and tofu casserole, 127
Maple walnut tofu ice cream, 48
Mayonnaise, 7
Metric equivalents, ix
Middle Eastern-style tempeh and aubergine stew, 98
Middle Eastern-style tempeh and okra stew, 99
Middle Eastern-style tempeh balls, 100
Millet and vegetable savoury, 128
Miso gravy 1, 113
Miso gravy 2, 114
Miso soup with cabbage and carrot, 107
Mock 'chicken', 15
Mock 'chicken' cooked Indonesian style, 17
Mock 'ham', 14
Moroccan-style tempeh brochettes, 102
Mulligatawny soup, 29
Mushroom bisque, 22

· O ·

Oaty tofu and bean crumble, 61

· P ·

Pancakes stuffed with bean milk sticks, 12
Peking noodles, 56
Pineapple cream, 40

· Q ·

Quantities, viii
Queen scones, 51

Quick pizza, 120

· R ·

Raspberry tofu ice cream, 49
Rhubarb fool, 43
Risi e bisi, 80

· S ·

Savoury tempeh and tofu loaf, 140
Savoury tempeh loaf, 95
Savoury tofu 'mince', 60
Smoked tofu and mashed potato cakes, 79
Smoked tofu charlotte, 77
Smoked tofu fritters, 72
Smoked tofu, lettuce and tomato sandwich, 71
Smoked tofu pasties, 75
Smokey bean fritters, 74
Soft cheese, 7
Soups:
    Chilled cream of cucumber, 26
    Cream of cauliflower and potato, 23
    Cream of celery, 25
    Cream of mushroom miso, 108
    Lentil and smoked tofu, 69
    Miso with cabbage and carrot, 107
    Mulligatawny, 29
    Mushroom bisque, 22
    Tofu gumbo, 28
    Tomato bisque, 24
    Vegetable with miso, 109
    Vichyssoise, 27
Soya 'cream cheese' spread, 110
Soya milk, 3
Soya milk skin, 9
Spaghetti milanese, 81
Spaghetti with tempeh sauce, 88
Spaghetti with tofu and miso sauce, 125
Spaghetti with tofu and peas, 38
Spiced pressed tofu, 64

Index

Spicey ricey casserole, 59
Spicy tofu with coconut sauce, 32
Spicy tofu scramble with red pepper and tomato, 36
Spreads:
    Devilled tofu and celery, 30
    Lentil and parsley, 111
    Soya cream cheese, 110
    Tahini, 111
    Tempeh, 132
    Tofu and miso, 123
Steamed savoury smoked tofu pudding, 76
Stir-fried bean milk sticks Shanghai-style, 11
Stir-fried rice with tempeh and tofu, 137
Strawberry 'cheese' dessert, 42
Swiss steak, 57

· T ·

Tahini spread, 111
Tahu goreng, 39
Tangy noodle casserole, 126
Tempeh croquettes with mushroom sauce, 91
Tempeh hash with potatoes, 94
Tempeh paprika, 139
Tempeh spread, 132
Tempeh stroganoff, 133
Tempeh stuffed peppers, 89
Tofu and green pepper dish, 54
Tofu and miso casserole, 124
Tofu and miso dip/spread, 123
Tofu and tempeh burgers, 138
Tofu french toast, 50
Tofu goulash, 62
Tofu gumbo soup, 28
Tofu knishes, 35
Tofu strudel, 44
Tomato bisque, 24

· V ·

Vegetable soup with miso, 109
Vegetable stew, 117
Vicyssoise, 27

· W ·

Warming winter stew, 130
Winter hodge podge, 70

· Y ·

Yoghurt, 5